My America

What My Country Means to Me

by 150 Americans from
All Walks of Life

Edited and with an Introduction by
HUGH DOWNS

A LISA DREW BOOK
SCRIBNER
NEW YORK   LONDON
TORONTO   SYDNEY   SINGAPORE

A LISA DREW BOOK/SCRIBNER
1230 Avenue of the Americas
New York, NY 10020

SCRIBNER and design are trademarks of Macmillan
Library Reference USA, Inc., used under license by
Simon & Schuster, the publisher of this work.

A LISA DREW BOOK is a trademark of
Simon & Schuster, Inc.

For information about special discounts for bulk
purchases, please contact Simon & Schuster
Special Sales: 1-800-456-6798
or business@simonandschuster.com

Designed by Colin Joh
Text set in Concorde
Manufactured in the United States of America

1 2 3 4 5 6 7 8 9 10

Library of Congress Cataloging-in-Publication Data is
available.

ISBN 0-7432-4089-8

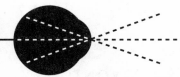

This Large Print Book carries the
Seal of Approval of N.A.V.H.

To my wife, Ruth, for uncountable ways

ACKNOWLEDGMENTS

Valued assistance in making this book a reality has come from a small number of people whose inspiration and encouragement, plus, in each case, skilled effort, were essential to the development of the work. I want to thank editor Lisa Drew, Bill Adler Jr., Erin Curler, Jeanne Welsh, and all those in the Adler offices and the production departments of the publisher, who were a joy to work with.

CONTENTS

CONTENTS

This work would never have seen the light of day without Bill Adler. He understood that in America's newfound sense of unity, people might wish both to express and to hear from others how they feel about the nation in light of the jarring events of September 11, 2001. My parallel thoughts about the book's prospects were bolstered by Bill's enthusiasm.

The range of various spectra in the responses—from mere reaction to thoughtful concern, from insightful opinion to more-or-less boilerplate jingoism, from philosophic overview to deep personal outrage—this variety I was not prepared for. Some of these essays are powerful and poetic. Some seem to reflect a stunned condition on the part of the contributor.

But all of them share a newborn or reawakened feeling about the country we live in—an underlying concern for it, whether that concern is rooted in anger and fear, or in a sensed and urgent need for action, or internal correction, or wagon-circling. Some are personal narratives that explain and justify the patriotism of the writer. Some examine and praise the values that make the country great.

I had my own feelings about the events on September 11 that woke us all up. But after reading all these essays I have amended to a certain extent how I feel about America. The articulated thoughts of this group of my fellow countrymen have brought a wider perspective to my own ideas and my own patriotism. Since a nation comprises its citizens and not just its geographic and material resources, it was of great value to me to hear from them, and it's my hope you will find it worthwhile to read what they have to say.

Like many of my countrymen I floated through years of taking for granted the environment of political freedom. I was vaguely aware of what the colonists had suffered under King George III and how the Founding Fathers had the guts to declare the colonies independent and the wisdom to forge a new government for a new country that would embody the values humanity strives for.

Even knowing the civics-lesson basics of these facts, I took our political freedom for granted. All the rights and privileges, all the protection and opportunity, I took as minimal condition for my function as a citizen until an incident a few years ago that brought home to me, powerfully, that I was a fool if I continued with this outlook.

My wife and I were in Romania for a broadcast segment on the *Today* show, during which I interviewed the then-new leader of the country, Nicolae Ceausescu. This unpleasant person, destined to lead his country into disaster and lose his life at the end of a tyrannical reign as dictator, bragged to me about his plans for the Romanians. He outlined better care for the aging, a renovation of the country's education system, and an almost Utopian future for the country. At some point in the ensuing years he went off the rails, abandoning those rosy plans to consolidate his grip on power until he had established one of the worst totalitarian regimes in history.

During this visit, we struck a friendship with a young poet—a girl whose father had been Romania's ambassador to the United Nations. She had lived in New York long enough to get a taste of America, going to school in the city and enjoying some success in writing in two languages. She was married to a writer, who had done some excellent research in geriatric medicine and published a book on the subject, which unfortunately was gutted by a government committee that sat in judgment on the ideological suitability of the contents. He was understandably frustrated and depressed. He chain-smoked and nursed an ulcer. They lived in a tiny apartment with her parents, and had almost no privacy. They would have loved to have come to the United States, but that was not possible. When our visit was over, they accompanied us to the airport. Before we boarded the plane, I saw a look in her eyes that stabbed me with a pain I had never felt before. I could see that she knew I had in my pocket an article of priceless value: a United States passport. Something deep inside me said, If I ever complain about the U.S. again—its bureaucracy, its red tape, its partisan bickering, its taxation—I hope someone kicks me soundly. Its bureaucracy is mild compared to that of almost anyplace else, its red tape is quite tolerable, its partisan bickering does not result in riots and gunfire, its taxation has full representation—there is nothing to complain about. Not when you put it all into the perspective of the human condition on this planet.

Alfred Lord Tennyson, in his "Hands All Round," wrote, "That man's the best Cosmopolite / Who loves his native country best."

You can love your neighborhood best if you love your city. And your city best if you love the state it's in—and so forth. If your love of country is not mere jingoism or chauvinism, you are free to consider alliances, blocs, coalitions, etc. So the hierarchy can continue to expand, and could, conceivably in future times, comprise aggregations of planets, and galactic federations and super-cluster empires. (Science fiction writers have loved this idea.) But at the moment the highest organizational entity that has enough stability to develop a history is the nation. Nations appear to have life spans that, in geologic time, are short—they seem to commit suicide after two or three centuries. If this is the historic norm, is it possible that there is a unique characteristic of the United States that may enable it to override this senescence that dooms nations—that in our self-correcting potential we have the secret of national immortality? The vitality of our Constitution lies in its machinery for amending itself, and even for reversing amendments that may prove useless or damaging. For the first time in history a quality has been added to self-government that might give it this ongoing self-preservation. Such a country deserves to be loved.

There are two reasons for loving the country you were born in, and have allegiance to: (1) It's what you're used to. The language, customs, cultural idioms, values, and overall environment are "the way things are," and the ways of others, tolerant though we may wish to be, are just not quite familiar. (It has been said that our standard of quality in drinking water is from the wells of our childhood.) And (2) the United States of America does have qualities that make it superior to any other country from the standpoint of values. (This of course depends on the criteria one tests with. Some years ago a study was conducted on what culture or nation or social entity provided the best opportunity for a happy life, and it turned out that for community support, care of the ill and the elderly, a protective environment for childhood, the percentage of waking time necessary to make a living, the degree of freedom from war and want, and the absence of abject poverty, the prize went to the Kalahari Bushmen of Africa. There have also been some American Indian tribes that would have scored high on this test.) But of the larger nations, I can't think of one that offers as much of an overall chance for happiness and a reasonable life expectancy as the United States does. Even our lower-middle-class citizens have more security, more and better food, more comfort, more recreation, more knowledge than monarchs of hundreds of years ago. The quality of our lives is owed in part to modernity.

Beyond the familiarity and convenience of feeling good about, and protective of, the United States—and feeling we have a duty of some sort to sell its structure and philosophy to other cultures—when we look at our overall tolerance of other faiths, other countries, other religions (don't we have them all within our own borders?), when we observe the good-heartedness of Americans, their reaction to a disaster anyplace in the world, or to a child in a well who has a chance of rescue, or to victims and their relatives, the American character is compassionate—perhaps more so than that of any other nation. This is a hallmark of superiority, if you're willing to define superiority my way.

The values we injected into the country at its birth are those the colonists brought and built on—the Pilgrims, who sought escape from religious persecution; the explorers who had the nerve to push into the unknown; the Founding Fathers, who preserved what was great about English Common Law, and had the wisdom to understand the necessity for checks and balances among branches of government, a bicameral legislative setup, a separation of church and state, and upholding the strange, always uneasy relationship of a federal government and the rights of individual states.

As hostile and aggressive as humans can be (and the extent of this trait is dreadful), there is a countervailing force of empathy, cooperation, and helpfulness, which is not as frequently reported as it ought to be, but without which there would never have been anything like civilization. These are the values that now, tragically, are under attack by zealots who have no regard for any values in this life, and who stake everything on the monolithic idea that a paradise awaits them if they destroy all who are not of their narrow belief.

It's possible that this kind of war, into which we were unwittingly forced, is as different as war became when gunpowder eliminated body armor and swords and lances. What form it will take is difficult to see with clarity this early in the struggle. It is grotesque.

But it is in the American character to expel a grotesque. We have overcome demagogues and dictator wannabes like Huey Long, or Joe McCarthy, ludicrous though dangerous episodes such as the Hessian mercenaries during the Revolution, Aaron Burr's attempt to set up a separate country at Blennerhassett Island, and Richard Nixon's possible tinkering with the idea that he might save his position by suspending the Constitution and protecting it by declaring martial law. We simply do not tolerate dangers of this sort, and we somehow (knock wood) always come up with a means to preserve our stability and the values we cherish.

Nostalgia is intensified when changes are abrupt. Memories of my childhood become somehow more vivid, and more American, if you will, than they had been a while back, before September 11.

I'm sure it's because of the shock of that day—the dismay of not seeing it coming, and the realization that we did not know how bitterly hated we had become, or why that hatred had developed and festered to such a pitch.

I had about as American a childhood as I can imagine. We were not wealthy, and several of my early years were characterized by no frills as far as material possessions or social status went. But we never went hungry, never found a reason to feel bitter about fate, the government, the neighbors. How my father kept us afloat during the Depression is still something of a mystery to me. There was no opportunity for him to pursue, and he put in long hours on the road as a salesman of tires and batteries, through an eight-county territory in northwestern Ohio. He got home in time for dinner (which we called "supper") about half the time. He put enough miles on his truck to go around the world three times.

When I was nine the family moved from the city of Lima, Ohio, to a small farm on the Spencerville

Road. We paid rent on seven acres, an old house, two barns, and a chicken house. There was an orchard with pear and apple trees, a field and a woods and a lake where my brothers and I learned to swim. We had a cow, sold milk and veal from the calves, raised chickens and ducks, along with small patches of tomatoes, potatoes, string beans, and sweet corn.

Two things I remember with increasing gratitude, even now, that my father did for me: He had an ancient Underwood typewriter, and I was fascinated to learn that there were people who could type words and sentences without looking at the keyboard. My father, who was not one of them, bought me a typing book and suggested I teach myself to touch-type. Within a year, this magic was mine, and to this day I type faster than I think—which is not to say much for either process—but it is a skill I cherish. The other gift from my father had to do with music. My parents were very much into classical music: operatic, symphonic, and chamber groups. We listened to this on phonograph records and on the radio, and it surely is the basis of my deep appreciation of good music. But when I was eleven, living in the country, I had friends who introduced me to country music—hill and folk songs, bluegrass, cowboy ballads and trail songs, and that American sound that began to permeate the music of some composers who wrote for large orchestras—such as Aaron Copland, Virgil Thomson, eventually Alan Hovhaness and John Williams—and I wanted a guitar.

My father, who had had absolutely no use for country-and-western music, waited until he saw I really wanted a guitar. This was something we could not afford. But in his rounds as a salesman, he found a six-string Spanish acoustic guitar that had come unglued at the fingerboard and required some fixing up. I don't know what he paid for it, but he brought it home and let me help him reglue the box. This he did with due diligence, because when strung and tuned up, a guitar suffers a lot of force, and a tendency to come unglued and collapse. I had listened to a musical group down the road—a family named Silver—who played guitar, mandolin, fiddle, and bass, and, to my inexperienced ear, produced a breathtakingly professional sound in the hillbilly genre. I put classical music on the shelf, but before I outgrew that guitar I was figuring some chords on it, and trying some melodic lines that fell outside the country-and-western framework.

My brothers and I had adventures in the fields and woods and around the lake that may not have rivaled Huck Finn's, but they set an American tone. We also attended a small country schoolhouse, MacBeth School, not quite the traditional one-room country school—it had two rooms. In one there was a teacher for the first, second, and third grades, and in the other for the fourth, fifth, and sixth.

The room in which our studies took place (fourth, fifth, and sixth grades) was dominated by a large woman who appeared middle-aged to me at the time (she was probably not yet forty)—a Mrs. Clem, who (I swear) spent the mornings reading from the Bible and Zane Grey, and the afternoons examining geography, arithmetic, history. Mrs. Clem apparently considered Zane Grey's works canonical scripture. It wasn't till I was much older that I began to realize both the weirdness of this, and the fact that Zane Grey was more than a pulp Western writer. One reading of *Tappan's Burro* shows that he wrote literature and not just pulp.

Am I any worse off for this mixture of church and state in my fifth-grade class? Or for soaking up the American spirit in the Zane Grey I listened to (and read years later)? I think not, even though I favor enough separation to ban prayers in schools.

I went by bus to a centralized school for grades seven through twelve, Shawnee Centralized School for junior high and high school. (The Shawnees were an important tribe in Ohio. Adopting Indian names was ironic—as though we Europeans who settled the land were the real tenants, and the natives who were here before us were merely here for the purpose of providing us with quaint names. When Chief Dan George, the Native American who briefly had an acting career in the movies, was asked to speak at a ceremony celebrating Canada's Centennial Year, he commenced by saying, "I find it amusing that you people think Canada is only a hundred years old.")

On reaching voting age I took pleasure in casting my vote, not so much because I thought it had real influence on the outcome of an election, but because I thought that to neglect the exercise of that famous franchise would cut me off from the country in a way I did not want. (Maybe it was the same kind of emotional motivation that causes me to finish what's on my plate—it's how I was brought up.) But I believed I was a citizen, and for the next sixty years I gave little thought to any need for concern about the nation's security—the safeguarding of not only its borders, but its values. The terrorist attacks of last year shook me into an awareness I now share with everyone else.

I invite you to share the awareness put down by the following messages from 150 contributors to this volume.

—Hugh Downs

ALAN ALDA

Alan Alda is an Emmy Award–winning actor, writer, and director.

As far as I know, I'm the grandson of an illegal immigrant. My father's father came here from Italy and simply never returned to the ship he had worked his way over on as a barber. My mother's grandparents came from Ireland–legally, I think, so I'm totally legit on that side of the family except for a brief stay in prison by one of my uncles.

From these humble and troubled beginnings I grew up to have a taste of that amazing success that is held out as a possibility to all of us in this country, but actually enjoyed by only a few of us.

I don't feel there was some huge mistake made in my achieving this success; I was talented . . . but I know that chance was definitely on my side. I had something else, too: confidence. By the time I was a child, my family took it for granted that we were Americans and because of that we were entitled to everything the country had to offer. As I grew up, I became less sure that that assumption could be held by every American. I've been thinking again about this lately.

Three weeks after the attack, I went down to ground zero with a handful of other actors, hoping to help raise the spirits of some of the people working there. Mainly, we were there just to listen to them and offer any support we could.

We went downtown by boat and walked the last two blocks to the plaza. I turned a corner and there was that numbing sight. Giant steel shards against the black sky. Firefighters, police, construction workers were climbing over the wreckage, trying to untangle that devastating monument to cruelty, looking for the remains of colleagues, sons, and brothers in the pile. They were men and women who had gathered from all over the country because they knew they were needed.

An ironworker came over to me and introduced himself. His name was Johnnie Bell. I can still see his face. He looked very tired, and he spoke softly, but he seemed to speak from deep in his heart. "It would be awful," he said, "if we lost this spirit of pulling together after all this gets cleaned up. We're one country now. It doesn't matter about religion or race or things like that. We gotta stay this way. I don't hear anybody saying that."

When you're standing there in that plaza of heroes, you want to help them any way you can. I promised Johnnie Bell that the next time I had a chance to say something in public I would say it for him.

Buzz Aldrin

A former NASA astronaut, Buzz Aldrin served as the pilot of Gemini XII *in November 1966. As the lunar module pilot of* Apollo XI *in July 1969, he and Neil Armstrong were the first humans to walk on the moon.*

For me, the greatness of America lies less in the bywords "freedom" and "equality" than in what those rights and privileges have allowed us to accomplish as a people. The history of America is one of restless idealism and a phenomenal readiness to work, of migrants and immigrants whose visions of a better life settled the West and raised up cities, of the miners, lumberjacks, cowpunchers, and prairie farmers who tamed the continent.

The genius of America has been that of its explorers, scientists, inventors, and builders—people with energy, curiosity, and imagination who were willing to take risks, people like the Wright brothers, in whose bicycle shop human flight was born; or Thomas Edison, the train boy and itinerant telegrapher whose incessant tinkering invented much of the twentieth century; or Washington Roebling, who after a permanent injury on the site directed the completion of his Brooklyn Bridge through a telescope from his sickroom; or Robert Goddard, the stooped, tubercular man who developed the first liquid-fuel rocket with a handful of helpers in the broiling New Mexico desert, never losing his Yankee optimism through decades of failure and "moon-man" ridicule. Or James J. Hill, who built the Great Northern Railroad, a rough-hewn, thickset, one-eyed man with a massive head and long, shaggy hair, who would climb down from his private railroad car in a blizzard to crawl under a stalled locomotive or relieve one of the older shovel-stiffs, all of whom he knew by first name. A frontier character in a frock coat, he captured the romantic image of rugged American expansion when he said, "Give me enough whiskey and enough Swedes and I'll build a railroad to Hell!"

The spirit of American progress and prosperity lies in its great projects—the bridges, canals, sky-scrapers, and transcontinental railroads, Roosevelt's arsenal of democracy, and Kennedy's mission to the moon. But the greatest of all projects has been America itself—the Great Experiment, John Winthrop's "City Upon a Hill," the last best hope of humanity.

If the moon landing epitomized the vision and energy at the heart of the whole American epic, it was also the harbinger of its future. We are alive at the dawn of a new Renaissance, a moment much like the morning of the Modern Age, when most of the globe lay deep in mystery. Yet government alone cannot launch a space-faring America. It will be the

Roeblings, Hills, and Robert Goddards of the twenty-first century who will make the difference. And in their wake, a new American dream will people the stars.

Shaun Alexander

Shaun Alexander, the University of Alabama's all-time rushing leader, with 3,565 yards in four seasons, is a running back for the Seattle Seahawks football team.

From the day I was born, my mom taught me two very important life lessons: 1) that living your life for the Lord will always bring many blessings, and 2) that I am blessed to be living in America.

On September 11, 2001, I was in my house in Seattle, Washington, sleeping. My old neighbor I grew up with, who is like a little brother to me, called and woke me up from his home in Florence, Kentucky. He told me that somebody just flew into the World Trade Center. Moments later, my older brother called me and told me the same thing. Realizing that it was no longer a dream, I jumped out of bed to turn on the news. At that moment, the second building was hit.

Immediately, I began to think about America. America to me has always been a place of freedom to make choices and an ability to be successful in whatever you do. From the beginning of our country, the Founding Fathers, though not perfect, founded this country on Jesus Christ. Knowing their decisions were based on the Lord has made our country blessed and prosperous.

Finding out that the people who drove the planes

into those buildings that day were enemies of America confused and assaulted me. My love and pain went out for my country, as my passion grew. Then the buildings began to collapse. That is when I remembered, just as our country has enemies, in my own faith, I have an adversary. We must always be prepared and ready for an attack from the enemy. Now more than ever, we must stand up in our faith and be proud to be Americans.

LINCOLN ALMOND

Lincoln Almond is governor of the state of Rhode Island.

There is a resilience that is typically American. It defines how we overcome challenges and how we look to the future. We are a remarkably diverse people who have combined our talents to build a truly great nation. We draw on our spirit to celebrate and nurture our freedoms, and, when necessary, we have rallied together to defend our way of life.

This new century has dawned with a horrible tragedy. As a nation, we have responded with an outpouring of support for the victims and their families and a resolve to preserve our liberty for future generations. We have unfurled our flag with a renewed sense of patriotism.

History teaches us that our response has many precedents. I was nine years old when the Second World War ended, yet I still have vivid memories of those who served and those who made the ultimate sacrifice. I also remember how everyone in my Central Falls, Rhode Island, neighborhood had a sense of purpose, a common goal, and a willingness to endure hardships. Virtually every American of that time shared similar memories. We have seen similar recognition of our common bonds in other times of national strife.

America's greatness is not found in our economy or

military capabilities; it is found in our people. As a free and diverse people, we often seem divided. In reality, behind our divisions lies a common commitment to the fundamental principles of our country and to each other. That commitment isn't always apparent, but when faced with adversity we have always come together. We are a resilient people.

BILL ANDERSON

Bill Anderson is a country music entertainer and member of the Country Music Hall of Fame. He hosted the country music game show Fandango.

In the early seventies, I cowrote and recorded a country music song called "Where Have All Our Heroes Gone?"

As the title implies, I was bemoaning the scarcity of heroes in modern-day America, chastising the "now generation" for focusing their sights on people whose hero status I questioned.

Conversely, I reminisced about the heroes of my generation, the Eisenhowers, the DiMaggios, the Stan Musials, John Waynes, and Gary Coopers, the good guys who wore white hats and said "yes sir" and "yes ma'am," "thank you," and "please." I conceded that there were a few current heroes worth emulating, the astronauts, for example, but I defied the listener to call even one by name.

My song was a success by all commercial standards, rising to number one on the popularity charts. Today, however, armed with the benefit of twenty-twenty hindsight, I realize (to paraphrase the title of another country song) that I was looking for heroes in all the wrong places.

Following the unconscionable events of September 2001, the word "hero" has been redefined for us all. I no longer seek my champions, nor urge others to seek theirs, in the money-grubbing world of sports, the artificial world of entertainment, or the hypocritical world of politics. I've come to realize that the *real* heroes aren't on a make-believe pedestal somewhere off in the distance, but rather they live next door to me, they work in the fire hall, the police station, or the hospital down the street. They volunteer in the soup kitchens and the nursing homes. They help feed, clothe, and love the children of drug addicts and AIDS victims. They read to the visually impaired. They lead our Scout troops and coach our Little League ball teams. They teach in our schools, they serve in our military.

Their names? That's not important. Their commitment and dedication, their unselfishness, their willingness to contribute, that's what matters. They are sometimes called to act in the face of adversity, to move in the face of fear, and they respond. That's what counts.

Where have all our heroes gone? Look around this great country we call America. There's probably one standing closer to you than you think.

WALTER ANDERSON

Walter Anderson is publisher, chairman, and CEO of Parade *magazine.*

A GOOD IDEA

One morning in March 1987, I was standing at a conference table in an official government office in Moscow. My wife, Loretta, and I had spent the previous two weeks traveling through five Communist cities in what was the first exchange to test a Soviet initiative for openness called *glasnost.* I was editor of *Parade* magazine. My Russian counterpart, who would later spend two weeks in my country, was Vitaly Korotich, editor of *Ogonyok.*

I had been introduced by a ranking Soviet official to his colleagues in the room and now the assembled group waited for me to speak.

What would I say?

Tell the truth, I told myself. But what *is* the truth? I am neither a diplomat nor a scholar. *What would I say?* I decided in that moment that I would say what I felt—because, at least for me, I was sure those words would be true.

I began by describing the kindness and hospitality that my wife and I had received from so many people, and I recounted how we were both moved by a particular war memorial, the compelling statue of a woman at Volgograd.

"Thus," I continued, "I'd like to help you to understand Americans, certainly not all but at least one—me. I am descended from anonymous ancestors who could have been poor people seeking riches, or zealots in a noble cause, or rabble-rousers fleeing some mischief, or worse. I really don't know who my people were further back than a generation or two. Like so many of my countrymen, I am a mongrel. We too have a statue, in New York Harbor, and she calls to people like me, patchwork ancestry and all. I have a bias, a deep, unyielding bias—favoring the guiding principles upon which my own nation has been founded."

Of course, I said more that day. But as I reflect now, since September 11, my own feelings about my nation have only been strengthened. History's most noble idea—that human beings of every ethnic stripe, all laying claim to their own faiths and beliefs, can live among and with each other, can come together and govern *themselves*—is a bright light that continues to inspire the restless, the abused, and the tormented to embark on the most courageous of journeys.

Tyrants never seem to get it: *Freedom* is a good idea.

MAYA ANGELOU

*Maya Angelou is a poet, writer, playwright, direc-
tor, and civil rights activist. She is the Z. Smith
Reynolds Professor of American Studies at Wake
Forest University, and is the author of numerous
best-selling books, including* And Still I Rise *and*
I Know Why the Caged Bird Sings.

For the first twenty years of my life I was an American because I was told I was an American. However, in my early twenties I went to Europe, visited
behind the Iron Curtain, and had my first introduction to Africa. On my way home, I realized that in
Europe I had become an American by choice.
Being an African American, the descendant of people who lived in some form of terror for three hundred years, I thought I had been toughened too
much to rock and reel and wobble by any new
assault. September 11 proved me wrong in my
assessment. The attack on my fellow Americans
and my country showed to me my own vulnerability, almost simultaneously. I was shown my strength
and the strength of my countrymen and women.

Yes, in those first few moments and even in the
first few days, we stumbled, we fumbled, and some
of us fell. However, in the first few moments there
were men and women who ran into blazing buildings never to exit alive, running to help other Americans, other human beings. And I must add, they

did so, these men and women who died in such glorious attempts, whether or not they could actually extricate any other person.

Their actions gave us the handholds we needed to pull ourselves up, so I have been an American by being born and then an American by choice. I am now a defiant American, defiantly.

PIERS ANTHONY

Piers Anthony is a fantasy and science fiction writer and creator of the Xanth fantasy series.

I'm an immigrant. I'm from England, and it was England I longed for as a child; America felt like exile. My parents did relief work in Spain during its savage civil war, feeding starving children, until my father was "disappeared" by the victorious dictatorship. He smuggled out a note, and with that and the threat of financial repercussions, they were able to get him free, though banished. Thus we came to America on the last commercial ship out, as World War II engulfed Europe. I don't like discrimination against immigrants; too many are far worse off than we were, victims of totalitarian abuses. America is a refuge.

I'm a writer. I write because my imagination will not be suppressed. America has the freedom for the flowering of the arts, including writing. When I write, I get love for my fiction and ire for my success. I understand what it is like to be the object of such mixed attentions.

I'm a naturalized American. My education, career, family, and future are here. I believe in the constitutional values, for I choose to subscribe to them, and wince when I see them abridged. Unfortunately there is some of that occurring now, as fanaticism, greed, and lust for power prosper in the name of patriotism. I do have a notion where that leads. Yet I hope and believe that in time America will cast off these illnesses and return to the grandeur of its aspirations.

America is relatively wealthy and free and proud, so is loved and hated regardless of its merits. Love inspires tolerance; hatred sponsors terrorism. I saw one building become a ghastly smokestack, and a plane crash into another like a deadly chicken coming home to roost, and I saw the tall towers fall. I saw the heroes and the bigots roused, and the shock of illusion shattered. I remembered the assassination of John Kennedy, the bombing of Pearl Harbor, and I thought of the Chinese curse: "May you live in interesting times."

I'm an immigrant. I'm a writer. I'm American.

DESI ARNAZ JR.

Desi Arnaz Jr. has starred in several television programs, plays, and movies, including The Mambo Kings, *in which he portrays his father, Desi Arnaz. He and his wife, Amy, operate the Boulder City Ballet Company in Nevada.*

My father's home was burned to the ground during the Cuban Revolution of 1933. His family lost everything and was exiled. Twenty-one years later, on October 3, 1954, when *I Love Lucy* was the number one show in America, my parents were guests on Ed Sullivan's TV show *Talk of the Town,* and here's what my father said:

> We came to this country and we didn't have a cent in our pockets. From cleaning canary cages to this night here in New York is a long ways. And I don't think there's any other country in the world that could give you that opportunity. I want to say thank you. Thank you, America, thank you.

What Dad said forty-eight years ago is still true today. We have the opportunity in America to pursue our God-given individual freedom—inner and outer. God gave each of us everything we need to grow into a responsible human being, and America provides each of us with endless opportunities for education, work, raising a family, and earning a living. And because America is an understanding and compassionate nation, even a person who once cleaned canary cages is given the opportunity to better his standard of living. Mom and Dad both exemplified what America stands for—hard work, accepting responsibility for yourself, and not blaming anyone else if your dreams aren't fulfilled—and the fruits of their labor are still loved and appreciated today because they were based on the honest, everlasting principles that made America what it is today.

Because America was founded on the godly virtues of life, liberty, and the pursuit of happiness, we will always be attacked inwardly and outwardly by those who hate us. Darkness hates the Light. Attacks will shake us outwardly but can't shake our inner spirit, because a strong spirit is untouchable and becomes even stronger through seeing evil. To see wrongness is to understand it, and through understanding comes strength. I rededicate myself daily to the lifelong task of seeing that there's nothing too low for evil to do in its attempts to destroy the Light. But evil can't win because the Light is strength and Light has already won.

I want to say *thank you, America,* for the opportunity you gave to my family and give to me each day. And I want to say *thank you, God,* for the physical beauty of our country and for this life. My allegiance to America and all it stands for is strong. I'm grateful to be an American and appreciate how blessed we all are to live in this country at this time.

ROBERT BALLARD

Robert Ballard is founder and president of the Institute for Exploration in Mystic, Connecticut. He is credited with the discovery of several shipwrecks, including the Titanic *in 1985 and the German battleship* Bismarck, *the lost fleet of Guadalcanal, and the American aircraft carrier* Yorktown, *sunk in the Battle of Midway in World War II.*

THESE ARE THE BEST OF TIMES AND THE WORST OF TIMES.

I have learned over the years that one can never get a true measure of an individual when times are good. It is when times are bad, when the chips are down, that you really learn about the depth of an individual, and that goes for a nation as well.

The sudden and violent death of so many innocent American people, so graphically broadcast live for all the world to see, was truly horrific. If there ever was a time in our history when running around crying "The sky is falling!" would have been justified, that was the moment. But we didn't.

Having grown up during World War II, in the shadow of Tom Brokaw's "Greatest Generation," and having watched my own generation tear itself apart over Vietnam, I have often wondered how "Generation X" would respond to its first trying moment.

Well, the jury is still out; our mission is not over. But from what I have seen so far, I am proud to be an American and I am reassured that our nation is in good hands, not only in the hands of those who presently hold the reins of power but in the hands of the next generation that will assume that responsibility in the years to come.

I am sleeping well each night. God bless America!

LISA BEAMER

Lisa Beamer is the widow of September 11 hero Todd Beamer and the founder of the Todd M. Beamer Foundation, created to give long-term assistance to victims of terrorism.

I have a distinct memory of learning the Pledge of Allegiance in Mrs. Charaper's kindergarten classroom. We stood with our right hands over our hearts and addressed the small flag hung on a wooden dowel over the chalkboard. As five-year-olds, we repeated the words until they were engraved in our memories. For the next twelve years, we said these words every morning to begin our school day.

It has been well over a decade since the pledge has been a regular part of my routine, but the words still ring in my mind:

> I pledge allegiance to the flag of the United States of America and to the republic for which it stands, one nation under God, indivisible, with liberty and justice for all.

It's a simple statement, but one that beautifully illustrates the basic tenets of our country. We believe in solidarity, faith, freedom, and fairness. As with any temporal organization, we are not perfect. We struggle to apply these beliefs to our real-life circumstances and dilemmas. Sometimes we lose sight of their value. Sometimes we get off track. But they remain at the core of who we are and what we do.

It is said that true character is shown in the moments of worst trial. As a nation, we endured one of our worst trials on September 11, 2001—an attack on our basic way of life, an attack on civilians on our own soil. What was the response of America? We showed solidarity in our drive to end terrorism and to support those who lost loved ones and businesses. We exercised faith in our leaders and in our God. We displayed a renewed commitment to freedom, even when this required personal sacrifice. We treated our fellow citizens and even citizens of our enemy's nations with fairness and concern.

I have always been proud to be an American. I have always appreciated the benefits that come with my citizenship. I strive now more than ever, though, to take seriously the responsibilities that come with that citizenship—to embody solidarity, faith, freedom, and fairness. Ensuring that these traits are at the core of each citizen will enable us to be the land of the free and the home of the brave for many generations to come.

YOGI BERRA

Yogi Berra is a baseball legend who played for the New York Yankees and the New York Mets. He is a three-time American League Most Valuable Player and was elected to the National Baseball Hall of Fame in 1972.

I've always felt real blessed, especially to live in this country. Everything good that's ever happened to me and my family is because of America.

If you dream and work hard, anything can happen here—I'm perfect proof. I became a ballplayer, which is all I ever wanted to be. Growing up in the Hill, a tight-knit Italian section in St. Louis, we didn't have a whole lot. My father, Pietro, had come here from northern Italy where things were real depressed. As for other immigrants, America promised hope, and he found work as a laborer in the brickyards. He brought my mother over, settled on Elizabeth Street, and had five children; I was the second youngest. Pop was from the Old Country and didn't know anything about this baseball business. My three brothers wanted to be ballplayers, too, but the family needed extra money—this was during the Depression—so they went to work. Me? I went to work, too, leaving school after the eighth grade. I was a tack-puller in a shoe factory, worked in a coal yard and on a Coca-Cola truck. But my brothers convinced Pop to give me a chance to play ball and pursue my dream.

My brothers were actually better than me, but they had to work and never got the chance. Years later when I was established on the Yankees, I told Pop that if he had also let my brothers play, he'd be a millionaire. He said, "Blame your mother."

My parents sacrificed a lot; so did my brothers. That's what America's about. When World War II broke out, everybody in the country sacrificed—it was the only thing to do. Our freedom and way of life were at stake. I enlisted in the navy and was sent overseas for duty on a rocket boat in the Normandy invasion. I was a gunner on a thirty-six-foot boat, part of a six-man crew. There were hundreds of ships in the invasion. The sky was lit with bombs and flares—it always sort of reminded me of the Fourth of July—and my commander told me to get my head down if I wanted to keep it. We worked like the devil to keep the boat moving and knock out the German gun emplacements. When the beachhead was secured, we knew the invasion was a success.

Serving this country was an honor, because it's an honor to live here. We're a country like no other. Sometimes we take things for granted living here. Not me. I owe everything to growing up and living in this country. I got a chance to do what I truly loved. I played baseball—the national pastime—for the greatest team in the greatest city in the world. I still swell with pride whenever I hear the national anthem.

To me, baseball is still the American game—it doesn't matter where you're from or what you look like or how little money you have. If you get a chance, you can succeed. To me, a kid from the Hill, it's given me everything I could ever hope for.

BRUCE C. BIRCH

Dr. Bruce C. Birch is dean and Woodrow W. and Mildred B. Miller Professor of Biblical Theology at Wesley Theological Seminary in Washington, D.C. During the days following the September 11, 2001, attacks, Dr. Birch worked with a team of psychologists and clergy helping the extensive White House staff cope with emotional and spiritual stress.

HOW SHALL WE SING?

It was when the nation was lost and the people were carried into Babylonian exile that the Psalmist lamented, "How shall we sing the Lord's song in a strange land?" (Psalm 137:4). Exile is not simply a matter of geography but is also a matter of spirit. In times of crisis some despair that singing—of joy, of hope, of renewal, of justice—is permanently lost in tears.

It is the teaching of the great religious traditions, as expressed in a multitude of cultural forms, that the divine power that enables life never allows death to have the final word. We remember what God has done, and we anticipate what God yet can do, and this frees us from the tyranny of the present when pain and loss grip us.

It is the great gift of these United States that when one voice is lost in a moment of tragedy—even a tragedy as deep and wounding as that September

Tuesday—an entire choir of voices stands ready to take up the song of hope and life. Every religion, every race, every ethnic tradition, every economic class, every age, every lifestyle is a part of the rich chorus of American life. In the crisis of terrorist attack, we have seen our nation sing in words of comfort and hope, in actions of courage and renewal, in resolve to justice and peace. In the face of violence and terror, we are clear that when even one suffers, all suffer. The renewal of our life's song as a nation must spring from the gifts of us all.

Terror imagines that it can divide and conquer. Terror imagines that it can create a world of us versus them. But at its best, the American vision encompasses all and refuses to narrow the boundaries of human community. This is why terror can never be fought only by raising our voices against external enemies. Terror must be rendered powerless by the renewal of singing that includes all voices in the chorus of our nation and the human family.

MICHAEL BLOOMBERG

Michael Bloomberg is mayor of the city of New York.

September 11 will certainly be remembered as the darkest day in the long and proud story that is New York City. Nearly 3,000 of our best and brightest were taken from us in the attacks on the World Trade Center, including 406 members of New York's uniformed personnel. But on that worst of days, we saw New York and America at our best.

In the aftermath of the attacks, our city's firefighters, police officers, and emergency medical technicians orchestrated the most successful rescue operation mission in history. They saved more than 25,000 lives, and set the courageous example that inspired the nation and became the spiritual foundation on which New York City began to rebuild. I am sure I speak for every American when I say that we will never forget them and what their sacrifice meant to our country.

On a recent visit to ground zero, I struggled with the question of what America means to me after the events of September 11. Ultimately, my mind settled on the words President Abraham Lincoln delivered in the Gettysburg Address on November 19, 1863.

In dedicating a portion of the Gettysburg battlefield for use as a cemetery, Lincoln spoke of his inability to further consecrate ground that had already been blessed by the sacrifice of the men who had died there fighting for the principles of freedom and equality. He stated that it was the duty of the living "to be dedicated here to the unfinished work which they . . . have thus far so nobly advanced."

I can think of no better way to describe the outlook of the American people as we embark on an uncertain path toward the future. In the face of extreme adversity, the American people have always responded with bravery and resilience. The same spirit that guided the soldiers at Gettysburg flowed through the rescuers of September 11, and it will be there as we rebuild New York City. That is what America means to me—the commitment to ensuring that, whatever the challenge, there will always be, in Lincoln's words, "a new birth of freedom."

BARBARA TAYLOR BRADFORD

*Barbara Taylor Bradford is an author. Her latest
novel is* Three Weeks in Paris.

I was in New York working to deadline on a book
when that most unwarranted and horrendous act of
war was perpetrated against America on September
11, 2001. Of course work stopped as I gazed in horror at the television screen, shocked, enraged, and
heartsick at the hideous events unfolding before
me. But in the next few days a new emotion entered
my consciousness: *pride.* Pride in America and in
Americans. In the most amazing way we united,
became one body of strength and solidarity
overnight. And quite unexpectedly I was carried
back to my childhood growing up in England during the Second World War. Most of that childhood
was spent crouched in an air-raid shelter or dodg-
ing Hitler's bombs on my way to school. But what I
suddenly remembered most was our unity and
determination to win the war. That is what sustained us during the Blitz, and it is these same
strengths that are sustaining us in America today.

With the attacks on America I truly came to
understand how much my adopted country means
to me, how much I love it and all that it stands for. I
am so proud to be a citizen of this fair land of ours,
the greatest nation in the world, where freedom,
democracy, justice, and fair play are the norm. How

wonderful it is to live in a land where women are honored and not denigrated, and where all voices can be heard. A land of hope and glory, where good opposes evil, and defeats it, a land of heroes and heroines, always ready to roll if that is what we have to do . . . Americans above all. Proud, patriotic, and unbowed. That's what my country means to me.

DAVID BRENNER

David Brenner is a comedian, best-selling author, and award-winning television writer, producer, and director.

I remember the day my fifth-grade teacher, Mrs. Bishop, told us that any boy could become president of the United States, and I thought, Sure, first you've got to be a man, not a woman, and a White Anglo-Saxon Protestant, not a Catholic, not a Jew, not a Hispanic, and definitely not a black. I remember looking around at my classmates in my poor Philadelphia public school and thinking of how not one of them would be president and how they would be lucky just to get out of the neighborhood.

I remember hearing every president elected in my lifetime make the same Inaugural Day speech about wiping out poverty, drugs, prejudice, bigotry, crime, governmental corruption, etc., how we Americans now under his leadership were heading for a "new America," and thinking that here we go again with four years of unfulfilled promises.

I remember watching the horror of September 11 and thinking, after the anger and sorrow subsided a little bit, anyway, about having traveled through about two-thirds of the countries around the world, and, although America is a land of broken political promises and unrealized, idealistic dreams, it is without a doubt the greatest country in the world, and, if not a land totally free for all its citizens, it is the most free, and whoever is elected president, although not "any boy," he is the leader of a special place, more special than any other.

I remember thinking, as I watched the House of Representatives run for their own safety from the anthrax scare, that, excluding them and others who are cowering, most Americans are citizens in the "land of the brave," and it is the common man and woman and child, if not the privileged, who make America great. I remember thinking about the firemen, the cops, the emergency workers of New York City, who thought only of saving lives, not of dying, and Mayor Giuliani, who called on all of us to continue living our lives in freedom and to live bravely, and I thought of how each of us must not give in to the enemies of our greatness as a nation, and we must not realize their goal of forcing us to stop living the American way of life.

I remember thinking about how proud I was of all those who stood, feet spread, looking deeply into the eyes of the terrorists of this world, and screaming, "Go to hell, and I'm going to help you get there!" It is this that I'll teach my three sons, none of whom will probably ever become president, who will listen to the same bullshit inaugural speeches, but each of whom possesses that special inner strength to live in the land of the free and the brave and fight to keep it that way.

I remember a Puerto Rican saying I read as a child, which translates as "Even the sun has spots, but its main characteristic is to give off light." This is my America, too, and what my country means to me.

DAVE BRUBECK

Dave Brubeck is a jazz pianist and composer.

September 11, 2001, was a day of awakening for all Americans, enjoying our prosperity and too caught up in a bottom-line mentality to pay much attention to what was happening on the other side of the world. In that hour of crisis, selfless heroes were born. Immediately, selfish pursuits were put aside and innate goodness went into action, ordinary people demonstrating in a thousand different ways compassion toward their fellow Americans. But we must learn to look outward as well as inward. We have now been forced to think globally about the needs of others and to acknowledge that we somehow must learn to share the abundance of Planet Earth. As surely as the treatment of Germany after World War I spawned a Hitler, our neglect and ignorance of the poverty and suffering of the Middle East allowed another despot to recruit the disillusioned and hopeless. When I recall the great generosity of the American people who fed a starving and beaten Europe and Japan after the bitter battles of World War II, I am hopeful that we will be enlightened enough to remember Christ's revolutionary message: "Love your enemies. Do good to those that hate you."

ART BUCHWALD

Art Buchwald is a Pulitzer prize–winning political humorist, journalist, and author.

My father was born in what may now be Czechoslovakia, but was then part of the Austro-Hungarian Empire. He didn't speak English and learned it from reading copies of the New York *Daily News* and the *Daily Mirror*, which people left on the subway.

As a first-generation American, I'm so pleased that he came here. Dad did not make a lot of money. He barely survived the Depression. But he appreciated, as did I, the opportunity that America could afford for anyone. I bless it every day. And I bless it even more since September 11. You have to see what's going on in the world to realize how lucky all of us are.

GEORGE BUSH

*George Bush was the forty-first president of the
United States.*

OUR COUNTRY

September 11 seems to have awakened us as a
nation—awakened us to both evil and good.

We once felt, protected by two oceans and two
friendly borders, that we were immune from attack.
But then we did not clearly understand the totality
of the evil that is international terrorism. We never
felt we would be targeted in such a brutal way.

Now the world, shocked by what happened on
September 11, has come together to wipe out the
radical cells that threaten us all, to find and bring to
justice the leaders of terror wherever they may hide.

In 1991 Saddam Hussein launched his brutal
aggression against Kuwait. Our goal of kicking the
invading forces out of Kuwait was clear. We knew
the enemy, knew where his forces were, and knew
that our coalition would succeed. But until our
superb military won a clear victory our country was
not totally united.

Today our nation is totally unified behind our
commander in chief as we face a far different
enemy.

We will again prevail; but the task is far more
complex. The enemy is as evil as Saddam Hussein,
but far more shadowy, his methods more insidious.

Though partisan politics has largely given way to the national good there will be partisan flare-ups on domestic issues. But I am confident that most Americans will continue to back the president as he leads us with strength and clarity of purpose in the all-out war against international terrorism.

The president is my son, so you can discount this proud father's words; but I know of this man's inner fiber and I know of the strength he gets from his faith. I know for certain that he is up to this tremendous task, and that he is blessed with a first-rate team.

We are a nation unified, determined—a nation now more proud than ever of our own freedom. We are a nation willing to assume the lead in helping all nations win out over terrorism.

We are strengthened by our faith. We are now proud to wave our flag and talk of patriotism. We are proud to salute our heroes. We are a great country, truly great when we are challenged.

We are the United States of America, stronger by far than we were early on that fateful morning, September 11, 2001.

Jeb Bush

John Ellis "Jeb" Bush is governor of the state of Florida and the brother of President George W. Bush.

My feelings about being an American have never been difficult to put into words. But in the last year, as our nation has suffered and been strengthened, it has become even easier to express my great love for our country.

The greatest strength of our nation is our people. The resolve of the military since September 11 to defend freedom has been remarkable and inspiring to me and to many others. Every state has answered the call to send troops to the cause, and I am proud that many Floridians are on active duty in the reserves. Another person who inspires me is Floridian CeeCee Lyles, one of the brave flight attendants who helped divert Flight 93 from attacking our nation's capital on that fateful day. The prayers, concerns, contributions, and volunteer efforts of Floridians and all Americans alike in the last year should give everyone confidence that America is a selfless and patriotic country.

Even though times have been difficult, the future of America has never been brighter. We are the leader of the free world and have answered the call to fight for those peoples whose freedoms are threatened. Our democratic system of government has proved that it can withstand challenges of many kinds. Our Constitution has been in effect longer than any other in the entire world. Our citizens continually demonstrate their strength of character.

In this new age of heightened security and awareness, it is even more important to reflect on the principles upon which our great nation was founded: life, liberty, and the pursuit of happiness. It is also crucial to spend time with family and to reach out to those less fortunate. Our liberty and our safety go hand in hand, and neither must ever be taken for granted. As the words of "America the Beautiful" poignantly express, Americans are "heroes proved in liberating strife, who more than self their country loved. . . ." Floridians love their country and will take inspiration from our heroes to make the future of America even brighter.

BENJAMIN J. CAYETANO

Benjamin J. Cayetano is governor of the state of Hawaii.

America has long prided itself on being the "melting pot" for people of various ethnicities. Nowhere is this more evident than in Hawaii, which boasts the most diverse population of any state in the nation with little of the racial strife reported in other areas. Our residents routinely cross the historically divisive lines of race, religion, and language in their sense of community. However, at certain times, there are no bridges to gap and no lines to be crossed. On September 11, 2001, we were all, first and foremost, Americans.

As we watched our country struggle to recover from the terrorist attacks, we vowed to preserve our ideals and way of life for future generations. Polls taken a few months later showed an upsurge of trust in public servants as we witnessed a president and a mayor answer an urgent call for leadership. Even more significantly, we saw hundreds of firefighters lose their lives in the line of duty. I felt privileged to be in public service at such a critical time in our history.

Many people would say that it is the "pursuit of happiness" that is distinctly American. This restless pursuit has led to amazing achievement that has defined us as a nation. At times it has also led to moral compromise, as individuals and government leaders sacrifice principles in the hunt for wealth or power.

The tragic events of September 11, 2001, afforded us the opportunity to reclaim some important values. We continue our pursuit of happiness, but, hopefully, with a clearer picture of what we are searching for. Ordinary people became heroes again and reminded us that this quest for happiness is linked to virtue, duty, and selflessness. Strangers reached out to those in need and reminded us that happiness arises from a sense of community and of responsibility for each other.

In Hawaii, we call this the aloha spirit, and it becomes an increasingly important part of our identity as Americans as we look to the future of our country with great pride and optimism.

*Margaret Cho is a comedian, writer, and creator
of the successful off-Broadway show*
I'm the One That I Want.

Somehow, saying "I am an American" makes me
think Uncle Sam is going to reach out and pat me
on the arm, the same hand he points with to show
me that he wants me, and patronizingly say, "Sure
you are, dear. . . ." When I say, "I am an American"
to my family, to my tribe, my culture, it reads, "I
want to be white." And in a way, I do. I want power.
I want privilege. I want double-lidded eyes and naturally curly hair and not to have to always tell people where I am from and to maybe someday hope to
appear in a costume drama. To act in one of those
elegant, sweeping film epics that are so lavishly
made about white history is one of the saddest
dreams in my life, as it may never happen, because
of the color of my skin and the insistence by the film
industry that Caucasians were the only ones around
in the past. And I'd like to not feel so alone in my
desire. One of the most heartbreaking things for
me, after September 11, was when CNN was running a series of spots, each one a brief eulogy of a
victim at the World Trade Center. They were mor-
bid, but infinitely modern, yet touching at the same
time, these commercials for the dead. One pictured
a young, good-looking Korean man, smiling, talking

about his brother, as if he were right there in the room with him. "He always acts like he's older than me, even though he knows I've got three years on him. He's just that responsible type of guy, you know. Taking care of business. That's my bro!" Screen fades to black, and then an image of the lost responsible one, with his name appearing slowly at the bottom. A Korean name, a Korean face. I wept despite my own cynicism. We were Americans too, and we were there, and we lost just as much as everyone else. It made me feel closer to all those nouveau patriots, waving their flags from their cars like diplomats, even though it was corny and just a way to recycle those old Lakers flag holders. It made me think, This is where my America lies. This is my country. And yet, the America that I turn to, while still longing to be proud and patriotic, is as frustrated and multicultural as myself. My America lies with the mosques all over L.A., and the world, besieged with hateful phone calls, mail, and graffiti, a convenient depository for hate, while the true enemy remained at large. My America lies with the postal workers, with two men already dead from inhalation anthrax, angry at the unjust, lackadaisical attempt at health care given to them as opposed to the outright hysteria on Capitol Hill. My America is the Flight 93 hero Mark Bingham, the all-American athlete, brave in giving up his life to save others, fighting the terrorists in the cockpit as the plane went down, the first soldier in the war against terrorism, and an openly gay man. My America is Arab Americans, getting hassled at the airport, unable to board flights, guilty of having the wrong last name. My America is about people volunteering to escort Muslim American women and children to school and to shopping, trying to give charity in the form of assurance. "I'm with you, you are going to be okay. You belong here."

What is so terrible about the attacks, the tragedy that goes along with all the death and destruction, is that it turns us against ourselves. The mysterious face, danger hidden behind race, peril and doom in cultures unfamiliar, unknown—the fears that come right down to us and them. It scares me. Because any of us could be next. Any of us who ever felt uncomfortable behind our face. What out country needs now is an escort to walk us to school, to shopping. Someone there to say, "I'm with you, you are going to be okay. You belong here."

DICK CLARK

Dick Clark, host of television favorite American Bandstand, Dick Clark's New Year's Rockin' Eve, *and* Bloopers, *is chairman and CEO of Dick Clark Productions, Inc.*

The other day, I was watching a television public service announcement. It was a conglomeration of people saying, "I am an American." The more I watched, the more I realized that it captured my thoughts about our country. The participants were representatives of every race, every size and shape, and all ages.

I've been lucky enough to travel extensively. What makes our country so unique is its composition. We live in a free society that draws from every country. That freedom has been paid for by thousands of young men and women who fought for our liberty.

Though we don't always agree with one another, our love of country is the thing that holds us together. We don't have a common religion. The things we eat have been introduced from all over the world. We vote differently from one another. We don't all look alike. We share a variety of tastes in art, literature, and music. This diversity is what makes us strong. There just is no place like the United States of America. It's one of a kind, and I'm proud to be an American.

JERRY COLANGELO

*Jerry Colangelo is CEO and owner of the Arizona
Diamondbacks and the Phoenix Suns.*

America has always been my beloved homeland,
which has served as an inspiration to me for its
ideals, traditions, and freedoms. I feel very blessed
to have been born in the U.S.A.–a grandchild of
Italian immigrants–and to have experienced the
blending of American-Italian heritage. America
represents a land of tremendous opportunity, which
now is an enormous melting pot of people of different races and ethnic backgrounds.

Diversity in our culture has impacted business,
education, medicine, science, and the arts. In the
short history of our country, we have experienced
independence, world wars, depressions, industrial
revolution, and the role as the leader of the free
world. This great country has allowed many to
achieve great heights in their chosen professions
because of the American infrastructure.

I love America with all my heart, and deeply
appreciate the freedom to worship and to raise my
family. September 11, 2001, and its devastation
served as a warning to all Americans–our homeland and our way of life has been attacked, and we
must stand tall and face the future with a fierce
determination to defend our country as never
before.

America will confront the coming years with a firm conviction to overcome the challenges and serve as the leader of the free world in new and exciting ways.

September 11 served as a reawakening of our faith in God and our national pride, and my prayer is that the reawakening becomes permanent in our lives.

God bless America!

STEPHEN COONTS

Stephen Coonts is a best-selling author of action-adventure thrillers.

The United States is a land of hope, a place where each of us has a historically unprecedented opportunity to choose how we live our life. We routinely ask children "What do you want to be when you grow up?" because we know that American youngsters truly are free to choose. American adults are too, and every year tens of thousands of Americans chuck the old career and venture forth in a new direction. As it happens, I'm on my third career now and, who knows, I may yet try another.

But in America the choices go far beyond colleges and jobs. America was built by people who believed they were responsible for themselves. Some would argue that in the age of the welfare state that view is dated, but even today few Americans are willing to abdicate their life decisions to a cult, sect, or charismatic leader. We refuse to have choices dictated to us because of our social, religious, racial, ethnic, or economic status. For good or ill, Americans freely choose their spouses, their friends, their religion, church, place of residence, image (all those advertisers get down and dirty here), recreation, charities, civic groups, how they will raise their children, who they will associate with, who they will vote for, the causes they think important . . . the list goes on and on.

The world is full of governments that try to control their citizens. In America it is the other way around, the citizens control the government. Our unique American constitutional right to bear arms, to own a rifle or shotgun and shoot the darn thing whenever we get the itch, defines us, I think, because it gives teeth to our right to revolt against tyranny.

For me, the symbol of all that is American is our freedom to fly. In America, average, middle-class folks can rent or own airplanes, can build one in their garage or backyard and get it licensed by the government and go flying. We can fly anywhere in the country with only a few common-sense restrictions, whenever we want to go. And every hamlet of any size has an airport with fuel for sale, a motel just down the road with clean sheets and hot water, and a restaurant that serves good food for a reasonable price.

This is my America, and I love it.

CATHERINE CRIER

Catherine Crier is the host of Crier Today,
a legal affairs show on television.

Even as a child, I dreamed of being an attorney. We
were a nation of laws, not men. These counselors
were magicians who could ensure justice. They were
the guardians of our precious freedoms. Without
them, tyranny or anarchy might creep into our
midst. After all, our founders told me so. Their Constitution and Bill of Rights had cast these roles.
These documents were our blueprints for a remarkable experiment in citizen government.

I'll wager these plans could not be drafted, much
less implemented, today. Why? Because our
founders were designing a nation, not a consor-
tium. Justice was the foundation. Freedom was the
promise. Equal opportunity was the path and *E
Pluribus Unum* the aspiration. A homeland for
democracy would be realized as others who cherished these ideals came to reinforce the American
experience.

At the Constitutional Convention, a woman
approached Benjamin Franklin and asked, "What
sort of government have we?" "A Republic,
madam," he replied. "If you can keep it." In recent
years we have faltered. Immigrants once came to
this land not to abandon their heritage and culture,
but to protect it under this glorious umbrella. Today

we are first African Americans, Hispanic, Jewish, Muslim, or gay Americans–a balkanized people who have elevated these differences far above the communal dreams.

We must remember that being an American is not the result of having a similar origin, religion, or blood. It is just a state of mind wherein liberty, equality, and justice are the principles worth fighting for. Although fragile and ethereal, these beliefs have sustained a nation for generations. Without them, we are merely sharing space.

After the attacks on September 11, real Americans were everywhere, but such character and spirit require more than flag-waving to sustain it. Values and principles are not just the stuff of history books to be dusted off as needed. They must be lived each day and taught to succeeding generations. Terrorists may threaten our bodies, but it is our hearts and minds that defend democracy. This horrific tragedy has reminded us of what we can be, what we must be, for the Republic to survive.

WALTER CRONKITE

Walter Cronkite is a veteran CBS news anchor.
His autobiography, A Reporter's Life,
was published in 1996.

The language is trite but the inspiration may not be as banal. To me my country is the land of opportunity, but not the land of economic opportunity through which I might expect to profit.

The opportunity that is America's is a still unfulfilled opportunity for leadership in a world crying out for help. Through the greatest of daring and the greatest of ambition this nation's Founding Fathers brought forth the design for a nearly perfect government that guaranteed the freedom and dignity of the individual. Perfection was denied, since, despite their high resolution to recognize and promote equality among all humankind, the economics and morals of the time permitted them to leave in existence the most abominable of inequality—the practice of slavery.

The government they devised, however, was a model of democracy. Thanks to the natural resources of the continent it eventually occupied and the geography that isolated it from deadly squabbles across the seas, it prospered until by the twentieth century it had become the world's richest and most powerful nation.

And that is where my belief in the opportunity for

this nation kicks in. It is our chance, at this vital junction of history's many streams, to use our resources to extend our opportunities to all humankind. With scarcely noticeable reduction in our wealth, we could extend a helping hand to the impoverished starving abroad. With scarcely noticeable limits on our profits, we could help stem disease around the world. With a dedication to international human rights, we could reduce the arms race to a fraction of its current costs. From our position as already the world's most heavily armed nation—and arms supplier to the world—we could lead the way in diverting those funds spent to develop and build ever more deadly weapons to the business of promoting peace—an effort that would include financing education of the world's ignorant, whose ignorance may be the most dangerous weapon of all.

This would be my America—the land of opportunity to lift the world to the next level of civilization.

VINCENT CURCIO

Vincent Curcio is the author of Chrysler: The Life and Times of an Automotive Genius.

America, to me, is not the feeling that pushes air to my lungs, color to my cheeks, or tears to my eyes. It is the fact of free thought, even if it is unpopular, wild, harsh, or unkind. If I want to speak my mind, I can—to myself, in the mirror, or to fourteen people on a street corner, or to millions on television. I can write my thoughts, too, without hiding them in the heel of my shoe, or behind the header of my car, or in a jar of export tomatoes. I don't have to pretend, either, that what I write is a children's fantasy or an allegory from the Greeks, to be decoded in fear by the like-minded and clever. You can do these things, too, and if you disagree, we can shout each other down in full voice. No iron will can mold my thoughts to its liking or pound what it does not like into dust. Yes, we can do these things in many democracies, but in this one, we could do them from its agrarian beginnings all the way up until now, the age of double-click. Through our history, even the people who tried to subvert this freedom did it in full light, for all to see and despise. I would die for nothing in this world, but on the right clean morning, when my breath is steady and my mind unclenched, I think that I could die for this. It is our happiest virtue and our proudest ideal.

CHARLIE DANIELS

Charlie Daniels is a Grammy and Country Music Association Award–winning musician. He formed the Charlie Daniels Band in 1970.

RETRO THOUGHT

The first things I remember are frosty Carolina mornings with a cheery fire crackling in my momma's big black wood cookstove. I remember snowflakes as big as goose feathers and a moon the color of newly made country butter and a night sky like diamonds against black velvet reaching from horizon to horizon.

I remember when the biggest problems in my barefoot life were sandspurs and red anthills. I remember Sunday school and "Kneel at the Cross" and trying to imagine what God looked like, Sunday dinner, short pants and haircuts and a little puppy my daddy brought home to me, and I remember love.

I remember sitting with my granddaddy on the front porch and watching the last of that magnificent southern sun bleed away into the twilight sky. I remember awesome steam-puffing ten-wheel locomotives, and the conductor's watch looking as big as one of my grandmother's biscuits.

I remember my mother smiling in a checkered dress, and Christmas always seeming so far away. Yes, I remember you, Carolina, grand old lady of the South, I remember you as home.

And now, the mighty four-lane interstates make their impersonal and hectic way where once the majestic longleaf pine stood tall and proud, and massive mills and factories belch their toxic smoke into an innocent blue sky. The empty storefronts on Main Street, U.S.A., are a stark reminder of the demise of the small family business and the advent of the monster shopping centers and discount stores with ten-acre parking lots.

Where once the family took the early evening air on the front porch, in conversation and fellowship, they now cringe behind locked doors in mute submission to the monolithic television set.

There was a time when a promise and a handshake constituted an honorable and unbreakable contract, and marriage meant forever, and children were raised with loving discipline, not the kind suggested in some book, but the kind gleaned and passed along through generations of nuclear family experience.

Now the little pristine streams where we freely drank the water are polluted. Political correctness takes the place of plain truth, and politicians are motivated by party doctrine and not the welfare of the nation.

Perhaps I'm just getting old and nostalgic, but it seems that if this is progress, the price is just too high.

God bless America.

MICHAEL E. DEBAKEY

Michael E. DeBakey, M.D., is chancellor emeritus of Baylor College of Medicine and director of the DeBakey Heart Center in Houston, Texas. Honors for his innovations in cardiovascular surgery include the Presidential Medal of Freedom with Distinction and the National Medal of Science.

The tragedy of September 11, 2001, at the World Trade Center in New York was cataclysmic in its enormity, not only for those linked immediately to the horror, but for all Americans and, indeed, all caring human beings. The impact of the jolt has manifested itself in a variety of emotions, from anger to revulsion, compassion, profound sadness, and apprehension. One positive effect has been a reawakening of a semidormant patriotism and a unification of an incipient societal splintering into single-interest groups. Suddenly, Americans felt a new appreciation for the unique advantages our country has to offer—freedom, relative security, and opportunity for fulfillment of each person's poten-tial. It is natural to become complacent when these advantages become commonplace, and therefore taken for granted. But the vast majority of the American people, in addition to being inordinately compassionate when tragedy strikes, will not toler-ate an attack on our nation. America is not only the land of the free but also the home of the brave. At such a time, all sociopolitical differences vanish, displaced by a determination to preserve and protect the ideals our country holds dear.

This, of course, is a different threat from any we have ever known, but Americans are versatile and creative when facing such challenges. Toward that end, the importance of dialogue cannot be overemphasized, so that differences can be openly discussed and resolved reasonably, fairly, and justly. When people are unable to communicate their positions persuasively and effectively, they may resort to physical expressions of their grievances, but rarely are the results positive or enduring. Such conflict is inevitably destructive. If we are to live harmoniously, whether in our neighborhood, community, nation, or the world, we must all strive to be fair, just, altruistic, and decent human beings, for only then will the human race not only survive, but prevail.

America has given my parents and me unusual opportunities. I have had optimal advantages in education and the pursuit of my professional interests. Because of the privilege of worldwide traveling, I have met, and interacted with, people of many different races, colors, ethnicities, and religions. All have a common desire for health, happiness, fulfillment, and peace on earth. That is also my own fervent hope for all peoples of the world.

Mark DeCarlo

Mark DeCarlo is an actor and a star of the
Jimmy Neutron: Boy Genius *movie and*
television series.

When you played for Benet Academy, you hated Montini High. Period.

Back in 1980, our bitter rivalry was the talk of Chicago's Western Suburban Conference. It even made the local paper. A 1–19 baseball season was fine, as long as Montini was the 1.

I loved the hate. It made me one of the guys, and provided great material for our dirty songs on the bus rides home–lots of funny things rhyme with "ini." And so it went for four glorious years. Then I moved away to the University of California, where I gained a whole new set of hates . . . unfortunately, not many funny things rhyme with "Trojans."

Years later, I was waiting out a blizzard on an airport bench in Denver, when a guy in a beat-up jacket caught my eye–a beat-up letterman's jacket–from Montini. I couldn't resist. I had a responsibility to my guys. I walked up and tapped the guy on the shoulder.

"We *hate* you guys." He turned around and scowled. He was bigger up close. A silent staring contest–I blinked, he won–then a glimmer of recognition in his eyes.

"Benet."

"You mean Conference Champs '78 through '80?" Sneer. Then, for some reason, I slapped him on the back and we both started laughing.

We spent the rest of the night in the airport bar, remembering our glory days. Pete—his name was Pete—was the guy who hit that triple in senior year that knocked us out of the state quarterfinals. It was a great poke—I watched from the bench as it sailed over the outfielders and smacked into the fence, missing a dinger by six inches. He remembered I was the guy who got hit with a shot put at that track meet and almost died. He played tennis with my cousins, and sat only three sections away from us at Wrigley. Turns out back in L.A., we lived only ten minutes from each other. He had just moved there and didn't know a lot of people, and imagine us running into each other way out here.

Back home, I introduced him to all my expatriate-Chicago pals, cosigned for his car, and found him a spot on my adult league ice hockey team. That's right, Benet and Montini, together, on one team. Put *that* in the paper.

Perspective and time—life is a succession of consciousness shifts, a series of crossroads. From twinkle, to toddler, to student, to teacher—the world doesn't change nearly as fast as we do ourselves. Through the ages, our survival has always depended on that. Just as it does today.

Our new road should start with the swift and

complete elimination of the evil at its source. These tumors must be removed wherever, and whenever, they flourish. But in the process, we cannot allow hate and evil to consume all that we are and have accomplished. To avenge our fallen, we must evolve . . . again.

It won't be easy. We're already DNA's most expressive, energetic, and self-aware species—the ones who mine the oceans and sail the stars. What more can we be? Perhaps the answer lies in who *we* already are.

Think about it. *They* are always the problem; *we* are fine. *We* are number one! In fact, some of my best friends are *we*. Without *them*, we'd be fine . . . right?

Sadly, it turns out there is no *them*. We're all *we*. Simply scratch the surface of the double helix—yet another cool thing we've figured out how to do—for the truth: *We* are all virtually identical. We're humans. Earthlings. Passengers on a little blue dot, hurtling through an incomprehensibly huge void, like squabbling kids on a runaway school bus.

God only knows where we're headed—but what *we* need to know is that the only way to get there . . . is together. Arriving safely, the only way we'll truly honor our heroes. Anything less leads to oblivion. The key to evolution . . . is survival. Just ask the dinosaurs.

So let the ashes of this evil feed our future. Let

their sacrifice be our ticket onto a better bus. Transform their slaughter into an auger that roots out the evil that divides us, and nourishes the goodness that unites us.

It's already churning in soup kitchens, flowing out of checkbooks, and skating on hockey rinks in southern California. The power of these effervescent bubbles of human spirit, stirred to life by inhuman acts, will combine to buoy us safely along our journey.

Or not.

It's really that simple. The toughest part of our trip will be remembering. Not now, not today, but for the years and decades to come, because this kind of change doesn't happen in a twinkling; only destruction happens like that. Everything good takes time. Remember how long it took you to realize your parents might not be total idiots after all? It's like that, only longer. A series of crossroads we must now navigate without them. To honor our heroes, we must *become* heroes.

We new heroes will treasure our bubbles and work to make more. We'll do things every day—big and small—to bring people together, rather than tear them apart. We'll do it so that we remember. And when we falter, we'll remind each other of all the sweet faces. All the dads missing at graduation. All the moms missing after school. And all the children . . . missing them.

It is possible.

Ordinary people can do extraordinary things.

You can make a difference.

All *we* have to do is . . . evolve.

Let's roll.

ALAN DERSHOWITZ

Alan Dershowitz is a lawyer and a Harvard Law School professor.

WE LEARN FROM OUR MISTAKES

The cataclysmic events of September 11, 2001, have once again reaffirmed that we, as Americans, learn from our mistakes. After it was learned that Muslim extremists had murdered so many innocent Americans, there was great concern that we might react in the racist manner by which we responded to the bombing of Pearl Harbor by the Japanese. Following that attack, we transferred more than 100,000 Japanese Americans—many of them citizens—to internment camps, far away from their homes on the West Coast. Many loyal Americans of Japanese ancestry lost their homes and businesses during this forced evacuation. The way we treated them shamed us all. Decades later we tried to compensate these victims of our racism by making token payments. But the real compensation was in the lesson we learned. Never again will we imprison entire ethnic, racial, or religious groups on the basis of the acts of a few.

We also learned from our mistakes during the First World War and the Civil War. During the First World War, we essentially suspended the First Amendment, imprisoning dissidents for simply opposing that war. During the Civil War, President

Lincoln suspended the writ of *habeas corpus*. Between the First and the Second World Wars we imposed racist restrictions on immigration, thereby dooming millions of Europeans to Hitler's gas chambers and ovens.

Although the Bush administration has called for the suspension of certain civil liberties—such as the right to trial by jury for non-citizen residents accused of terrorism—we have not seen any call for wholesale abrogation of the Bill of Rights in response to the current crisis. Despite the ill-conceived statement by Attorney General Ashcroft suggesting that those who disagree with him are aiding the terrorists, dissent has been vigorous and open. Virtually all Americans support our battle against terrorism, though many disagree with certain tactics and approaches. We are a healthy democracy in the throes of a crisis that will not soon end. We must always remember what distinguishes us from those who would destroy us: We are a nation under law, conceived in liberty, and dedicated to the proposition that all people must be treated equally. We must fight terrorism effectively, for it is the enemy of freedom. But we can wage this war within the rule of law and without violating our core freedoms. This generation of Americans has learned from the mistakes of our predecessors. Let us hope that our children and grandchildren will not have to learn from our mistakes.

ANITA DIAMANT

Anita Diamant is a writer and award-winning journalist. She is the author of the best-selling The Red Tent.

MY FIRST FLAG

My parents were immigrants, Jewish survivors of the Holocaust. They came to the United States after World War II, so I grew up seeing America through the eyes of newcomers.

As a child, I remember my father marveling about the total absence of "identity papers" in the United States. I remember his delight in the wide-open spaces of Colorado—miles of prairie and mountain, unfenced and free. Both my parents relished long, passionate political debates: Who's the better candidate for president/senator/mayor? How can the richest nation in the world fail to provide health care for its citizens? Why do so many Americans settle for Wonder Bread? (My daughter, following her grandparents' example, writes letters to the editor, circulates petitions, speaks out for the underdog.)

My own sense of patriotism was forged during the 1960s, and remains tempered by a healthy skepticism. America has yet to fulfill its founding promises of equality and freedom within our own borders. Nor has this nation lived up to its stated values in the way our government conducts foreign policy.

Yet, it is precisely America's promises and values that require me to honor and uphold my country's best self—a self still in the making.

And so, in the wake of 9/11, I put a flag decal on my car.

It is my first flag. I fly it in sympathy for those who died. I fly it in tribute to those who helped and continue to help, proving that love truly is stronger than death. I fly it as a pledge to an American future that lives up to the promises and values that continue to inspire the world.

PHYLLIS DILLER

Phyllis Diller is a comedian, actress, author, and recording artist. Lauded for her role as Dolly Gallagher Levi in Broadway's Hello, Dolly!, *she has received several awards for her professional and humanitarian endeavors.*

All you have to do to realize that we live in the world's greatest country is travel. No matter how imperfectly we muddle along, it's better than any other country.

Our forefathers were such swell guys with such well-founded ideas of what a government is supposed to do and what it has no right to do, that even with an occasional bleep, the United States of America is *the* place to live.

PETER C. DOHERTY

Peter C. Doherty was awarded the 1996 Nobel Prize in Medicine for discoveries concerning the specificity of the cell-mediated immune defense. He continues his research at the St. Jude Children's Research Hospital Immunology Department in Memphis, Tennessee.

MAKING HAPPY FAMILIES

The genomic revolution that has been supported largely by American and European taxpayers is telling us very clearly that the biological differences between various human populations are minimal. There are (for instance) only 6 of some 30,000 human genes that are thought to influence skin color. The molecular archaeologists of the genome tell us that, if we go back 100,000 years or so, each of us is "out of Africa." Genetically, we are all part of the one family. Culturally, we are much more diverse. This is also true for opportunity in the different regions of this small planet.

No family can be truly happy if there is not a degree of fairness. The challenge facing thinking people who live in prosperous, free, and open societies like the United States is to work out how at least a measure of these benefits can be extended to the rest of humanity. What we have been confronting very directly over the past few months is the realization that many people throughout the world experience lives that are mired in superstition, ignorance, and profound poverty of both mind and body. Hatred is the natural child of deprivation and hopelessness. How is this to be countered? What can we do?

Paradoxically, the greatest civilizing influence of the United States has tended to follow the effective use of military power. We saw this with the Marshall Plan in Europe, the reforms instituted by General MacArthur in Japan, the resolution of the situation in Bosnia, and now the defeat of the Taliban. In some situations, only the military might of a superpower can bring the stability that allows effective institutions to develop and flourish. The lesson that we have learned recently yet again is that any tendency toward isolationism and disengagement is very dangerous.

There are many other areas that we can explore, or are exploring, as we seek to live in a world that is safer, more prosperous, and more tolerant. An emerging international threat is the social destabilization caused by the appalling tragedy of the AIDS pandemic, particularly in Africa. Every American should take enormous pride in the tremendous effort that is being made to discover and disseminate better AIDS treatments and to develop an effective AIDS vaccine. When the history of this time is written, will the American lesson be that true greatness and compassion go together?

DUFFY DYER

Don Robert "Duffy" Dyer began his major league baseball career with the New York Mets in 1968. He also played for the Pittsburgh Pirates, Montreal Expos, and Detroit Tigers.

As a child I remember studying about Pearl Harbor and how it changed the history of America. I recall my parents telling me how the bombing affected their lives and the lives of every American, and how proud they were that each American stood tall and did their small part in helping America defend her freedom.

On September 11, I, like most Americans, was stunned by the destruction of the World Trade Center. For many hours I could not believe what I was seeing and hearing. The loss of lives and injuries to so many innocent people was too much to comprehend. As I continued to watch I began to hear about the brave people who were doing all they could to try to save lives and, while putting themselves in danger, help in any way possible. That is when I felt so proud to be an American and I wanted to help in any way I could, just as my parents did after Pearl Harbor.

Because this catastrophe happened on our own, home soil, all Americans feel much more vulnerable than ever before, and we realize that we cannot take our security for granted. We must all make some sacrifices to secure our country and the safety of all Americans.

On opening day in 1973, the New York Mets honored a number of POWs who had just returned from Vietnam by having them throw out the first pitch before the start of the game. As the catcher I was thrilled to receive the pitches. That night at a dinner honoring the POWs, I had a chance to talk to some of them personally, and I then realized firsthand what they went through to protect our freedom.

To me the destruction of the World Trade Center is the most memorable event in my lifetime, and although I wish it had never happened, I feel America will become stronger and a greater nation than ever before. I already can see and feel how proud Americans have become, how we have united together to back our president and our military forces.

As a baseball player I have had the honor of hearing the national anthem thousands of times before games, but never has it meant so much as it does now. I am proud to say I get goose bumps every time I hear it, and I can feel the pride and the patriotism of all the players and fans in the stands. It gives me a warm feeling to know that we Americans are ready and able to defend our freedom and our way of life. I now hold my head a little higher, the lump in my throat is a little bigger, and my colors are a little truer.

MICHAEL D. EISNER

Michael D. Eisner is chairman and CEO of the Walt Disney Company.

There are forty-five words that sum up what makes America strong, what makes America unique, and what made it possible for this particular American to come into existence.

There are forty-five words that draw people from all over the world, people like my family more than a hundred years ago, to America.

There are forty-five words that make it possible for every American to be whatever kind of American he or she wishes to be.

There are forty-five words that allow us to tell the government what to think rather than the other way around.

There are forty-five words that put into law something that goes beyond even the Ten Commandments. God may have created the Ten Commandments, ordaining a moral code for us all to live by, but man created these forty-five words, placing on each American's shoulders the responsibility to freely choose for him or herself:

"Congress shall make no law respecting an establishment of religion, or prohibiting the free exercise thereof; or abridging the freedom of speech, or of the press; or the right of the people peaceably to assemble, and to petition the government for a redress of grievances."

Forty-five miraculous words—the First Amendment of the Constitution of the United States of America.

JOHN ENGLER

John Engler is governor of the state of Michigan.

Since its founding, America has always stood for family, faith, and freedom. More than any other country, America has opened its arms to immigrants from around the world. We come from many different faiths—Jewish, Christian, Muslim. But we are all Americans. And as Americans, when we are tested, we close ranks and stand shoulder to shoulder.

Our generation, regrettably, has had its own "date which will live in infamy." The losses due to the terrorists and those who've harbored them are beyond comprehension. These acts of mass murder have seared our hearts—but they have also strengthened our resilience and steeled our resolve.

Throughout our history, Americans have turned to God in times of war. During the American Revolution, the Continental Congress asked patriots in the thirteen colonies to pray for wisdom in *forming* a nation. During the Civil War, President Lincoln asked Americans to pray for wisdom in *preserving* a nation. And President Bush has called on Americans to pray for wisdom in *defending* our nation.

In our nation's first great test, the American Revolution, Samuel Adams urged fellow patriots: "Contemplate the mangled bodies of your countrymen, and then say, 'What should be the reward of such sacrifices?'"

For more than two centuries, America has had an answer to that question—an answer that has inspired millions of people around the world. The answer is freedom. America stands for freedom. To be an American means to be free.

The victims of the September massacres did not choose to become casualties in a war with the enemies of freedom. So as our nation mourns, our solemn obligation to the victims is that we shall never, never forget. Likewise, as survivors, our duty is to ensure that our generation and those that follow shall live in an America that remains the land of the free and home of the brave—a beacon of liberty and justice for all.

God bless America.

STEVEN ENGLUND

Steven Englund is a writer, and the author of the
forthcoming Napoleon Bonaparte.

Living abroad keeps one keenly aware of his nationality, and the events of September 11 only redoubled that sense in me. Without any question, the first thing that leaps to my mind is the utterly unexpected reaction by the French to the tragedy. In four decades of studying this country and its history, including twelve years of living in Paris, I have never seen such an outpouring for America and Americans. Not only did I receive at least two dozen telephone calls from individuals (often just acquaintances) to assure me of their horror and concern, but many French publications known for taking a sharply critical view of U.S. policy and American culture and values declared themselves in solidarity with *Le Monde,* the great French daily, when, on September 12, it wrote, *"Nous sommes tous américains."* Even in subsequent months, the French reaction has deeply touched me and reminded me of how much goodwill America can also generate, alongside the more ambivalent feelings our power arouses in foreigners.

The French, of course, have an old democracy and a brilliant culture, and are rightly proud of many of their attainments, values, and institutions. A good example is how seriously France takes the life of the mind—writing, scholarship, the arts. A leading social philosopher recently passed away, and his death received a banner headline in the leading French daily, *Le Monde.* That would not happen at home in the States. No less important, French society offers better protections than ours for the poor, the elderly, the marginalized, and for temporary victims of capitalist competition.

On the other hand, America has uniquely developed certain traditions and attitudes that are outstanding: first, our greater freedom of choice and possibility; second, our capacity for good faith; and finally, our openness (however reluctant) to self-criticism. I constantly encounter here a deep-seated (if unconscious) cynicism about human nature, in general, and the prospects for an uncorrupt or fair political society, in particular. America, even in this era of skepticism and disgust about politicians and politics, continues as a society to debate its ideals, to hold itself to idealistic standards, and to generate within itself thoroughgoing criticism when those ideals are not met or are betrayed. We impeach a Richard Nixon at the height of his popularity and success. The French tend to shrug and regard his undermining of the U.S. Constitution as "par for the course."

America remains the only superpower, a role that is not one that any state has ever played (or will ever play) to the world's satisfaction, and the U.S. is no exception. But when I reflect on others that have played it historically—Rome, Great Britain, France, the U.S.S.R., etc.—I cannot but conclude that the U.S. fulfills the part with a sincere idealism, with a self-critical effort to be open-minded, fair, and to attend to other (including divergent and hostile) opinion, which may be entirely "inadequate," when judged by our opponents, but which, nonetheless, are unique in history, speak well for the United States of America, and bode well for the world.

BARBARA FAIRCHILD

Barbara Fairchild is a country music singer.

My husband, Roy Morris, and I have been doing a special production for the past three years to honor our veterans and to call America back to her foundations. We have stressed the need to return to patriotism and the values that have made our country great for so many years. I have always been proud to be an American and love my country so much!

The attacks on September 11 didn't fill me with fear. They filled me with courage, and I found my faith strengthened and a new resolve to be the best citizen that I can be. I encourage every American to take a look at what a gift freedom is and to hold fast to these blessings afforded us in our wonderful homeland!

Our president, our leaders, and our brave military troops who are on the front lines need our unwavering support for the days, months, and possibly years ahead, and our enemies need to see the same strength in the eyes of each American that we see in the powerful eagle that represents us. We must stay as determined to remain as our enemies are to destroy us.

JAMIE FARR

Jamie Farr is an actor. He starred as Corporal Max Klinger on the television series M*A*S*H.

I was born in 1934 in Toledo, Ohio, and my birth name was Jameel Farah. My name is an Arabic name. Jameel means handsome and Farah means joy. The world knows me under another name, Jamie Farr. I guess Jamie means Max and Farr means Klinger because that is my celebrated name and celebrated character I played in the wonderful television series *M*A*S*H*. I am of Lebanese descent. My father was born in Lebanon and arrived at Ellis Island in the early 1900s. His mother and father were both Lebanese. My mother was born in Cedar Rapids, Iowa, and her mother and father were Lebanese. So that means I am Lebanese on both sides of my parents. Today most people refer to us as Arab Americans. I challenge that description. I am not an Arab American. I am an *American Arab*. It is important for me to differentiate the two descriptions. I believe I should be called an American first and then attach my heritage. I am proud to be an American . . . I served in the armed forces . . . I have voted in every election since I became age-eligible. I salute the American flag and always pledge allegiance to it when expected. I anger when I see or hear of anyone desecrating the Stars and Stripes. I love America, yes, even with all of its true or false criticisms. I love America. God bless America. Yours truly, an *American Arab*.

MIKE FARRELL

Mike Farrell is an actor, best known for his role as Captain B. J. Hunnicutt in the television series M*A*S*H, many episodes of which he wrote and directed.

The terrorist attacks of September 11 and our response create a defining moment for America. The ensuing surge of fear and rage—understandable given a hideous act of wanton destruction—leaves little room for careful consideration of the consequence of actions taken under the influence.

Grieving needs time to reconcile the new reality. In that space, police, firefighters, survivors, neighbors, and others who so inspired on the awful day—reconfiguring the image of American hero—responded appropriately. When bleeding occurs, tend to the wound, as both a physical and metaphorical act of healing.

But care must be taken with grief. The impulse to immediately strike back at one's antagonist, despite common belief, has no part in healing and creates unintended consequences, often to the injured.

Leadership's pause before launch was a moment of hope. Had the opportunity been seized, the world's greatest power could have enlisted the United Nations, inspired the civilized community to condemn a crime against humanity, and demand an appropriate international response. In a single stroke we would have established the UN's proper role, demonstrated the United States' commitment to international law, and garnered the undying respect of the world.

But simplistic nationalism trumped thoughtful leadership and declared crusade. Six-gun justice . . . wanted dead or alive . . . with us or with the terrorists . . . Thus the din of bombs and wounded shrieks of defenseless people become white noise muted by flapping flags and blaring horns as thousands die because thousands died.

The world will never be the same, it's said, the implied arrogance suggesting that nothing matters to us but us. The destitute, the shamed, the hopeless—victims of terrorism for generations—look up, then back to a world always the same.

Abroad, brutes replace brutes. At home, fear congeals, rights die. Jingo redefines patriot. Speech becomes dangerous: "Watch what you say." The cliché that a chance to vote on it means Americans would repeal the Bill of Rights is tested; fearful, we fail.

Muted protests rise, are stifled, rise again. Collateral damage, tiger cages, lip service to values, addiction to violence, allegiance to oil, death to the innocent. Is this what we fight to preserve?

Who are you, America?

JOSÉ FELICIANO

José Feliciano is a Grammy Award–winning guitarist and singer.

America, my home, has *always* had an important place in my heart. When my parents brought me here as a child of five, I knew, by their confidence, that America was the answer to their prayer for survival.

My interpretation of our national anthem in 1968 was my personal offering in thanksgiving for what America had done for my family and me. Throughout the years following the misunderstanding of my version and the subsequent controversy, and along with my constant travel around the world, I can say with the same confidence that America is truly "a beacon of freedom and opportunity" for people everywhere. This title, however, seems not to be possible without criticism—even, at times, conflict. So when our mettle is tested, we must be willing to come together as a people, regardless of our differences. We must band together in solidarity, for as a nation, there has never been an equal, and as a people, there will never be a dilemma that we cannot overcome.

God bless America.

STEVE FORBES

Steve Forbes is president, CEO, and editor in chief of Forbes *magazine and a former U.S. presidential candidate.*

AMERICA'S NEW SENSE OF DESTINY

"With all thy getting get understanding." The great danger of our age is to be lulled to sleep by the anesthesia of abundance. To have so much yet mean so little. To move so fast that we have no time to savor life's sweet and simple pleasures. To let things temporal crowd out things eternal. To be too busy for those we love so that someday we are gone, or they are, before we acquire the good sense to slow down and extract the precious from the worthless.

On September 11, time stood still.

The bullet train of American life came screeching to a halt. In the blink of an eye, as we stared into the heart of darkness, that which is trivial suddenly gave way to the transcendent. We found ourselves letting go of the private, petty worries that can too often clutter our modern minds, and holding fast to the things that matter most.

Our almost defiant sense of independence suddenly seemed out of place and ill considered, and it quickly melted into a Mayberry-esque sense of interdependence, where life is about family and friends and a community that rushes in to help souls in need and then gathers at the barber shop on Main Street to take stock.

We called people in New York and Washington with whom we hadn't spoken in years, just to make sure they were safe. We turned not just to friends and neighbors but to complete strangers for strength and solace and moment-to-moment reality checks. We witnessed a geyser of can-do American compassion. And many drew closer to a loving, eternal, personal God who promises to walk with us through the valley of the shadow of death.

War is a crucible. The heat of battle is a great revealer of the hearts of men and nations. And in this first war of the twenty-first century, some truths have been revealed. Americans have, I believe, a new sense of destiny, a new seriousness of purpose. We are discovering anew who we are and why we were put on this planet and blessed with such freedom and fortune.

To cherish life.
To be a shining city on a hill.
To rally the great forces of good.
To triumph over the dark forces of evil.
To be an island of freedom in a sea of fear.
To do justice and love mercy and walk humbly
    with our God.

How has America changed? Only time will tell. But to paraphrase Churchill, let us therefore brace ourselves to our duties and so bear ourselves that, if the American nation lasts for a thousand years, men will still say, "This was her finest hour."

M. J. "Mike" Foster Jr.

M. J. "Mike" Foster Jr. is governor of the state of Louisiana.

Every so often, history reminds us that we should never take anything for granted, and it is during these times that we recognize our vulnerability. This horrible tragedy reminds me that there are evil people in this world who seek nothing but death and destruction simply because they are jealous of our freedom. In spite of the fact that we have all become highly aware and concerned about the possibility of future attacks, we must forge ahead with renewed vigor and prove to the rest of the world that the fire of the United States will never be extinguished.

Additionally, we must keep in mind that we all come from diverse backgrounds, and as Americans, we are bonded together by freedom and liberty. As Abraham Lincoln said, when this nation faced its greatest challenge, "Government of the people, by the people, and for the people, shall not perish from the earth," we too must embrace the patriotic spirit of our forefathers as well as those men and women who have given their lives to preserve the freedoms we cherish.

We have the opportunity to rise up even higher and lead other nations through this brave new world, and rest assured that we will be victorious in the war against terrorism. The events of September 11, 2001, will always be deeply entrenched in the memories of Americans, and, from that day, we as a nation have changed for the better. God bless America!

DAN GABLE

Nineteen seventy-two Olympic gold medalist Dan Gable is the University of Iowa's all-time most winning wrestling coach, serving from 1977 to 1997. He promotes the sport of wrestling and coaches potential Olympic wrestlers.

Being prepared is something one always values throughout one's lifetime. It means preventing the things that are not wanted and conquering the many things that are sought after. When one's guard is let down, vulnerability is the result. Why we become vulnerable is a reflection of our long-standing feelings of security. One must not be fooled into security. Even when things have gone well for long periods, one must be doing the right things that need to be done to remain well. America was brought up under this concept, yet our guard was let down on September 11, 2001. Of course this woke us up again, yet what a price to pay to get going to where we need to be again. Hopefully that will happen in the near future. America stands for being prepared and secure, and once we get there again, let's never let our guard down. America leads and is a symbol for the rest of the world. We can't afford any more major setbacks.

JOE GARAGIOLA

Joe Garagiola was catcher for the St. Louis Cardinals. He also played for the Pittsburgh Pirates, the Chicago Cubs, and the New York Giants, and went on to become a nationally known sports broadcaster.

I like a simple message. I'm always reading billboards and license plates looking for one with a clever way to give me a message I need to hear. After the events of September 11, there were plenty of messages simple enough to put on a billboard or a bumper sticker. But I didn't need to be convinced of "God Bless America"; that was already in my heart. In fact, it reminded me of the reasons why my father came to this country from Italy many years ago, reasons that were as valid then as they are today.

To my father, America was blessed beyond anything he could have dreamed. He came here without any doubt that he could make a better life for his wife and the children they would have. He was so sure of it that he made a big sacrifice—he came to America alone because there was only enough money for one to get on the boat. He worked and saved and waited out World War I until he could send for his wife six years later. But he knew it would be worth any hardship to raise his children in America and to become a *cittadino,* the Italian word for citizen.

I remember the many nights he studied for the test that would take him down the road to becoming an official American. But he didn't have to recite the Bill of Rights or tell me about the Constitution because he lived it. He worked hard, went to church, sent his kids to school—all the things that to him meant being an American. America still means all of these things for people in countries all over the world. Sure, we lived in an Italian neighborhood and Papa spoke Italian with his friends, but he learned to speak English with pride, and even if you didn't ask him, he'd tell you he was an American. He was proud of his new home.

Of all the messages sent to Americans after September 11, the one that said the most to me was a billboard of the American flag with the words "These Colors Don't Run." It reminded me that our great country will always face up to its responsibilities and do the right thing regardless of the price. That's the kind of pride and feeling I see in America since September 11. When people get together, whether at a baseball or football game or watching the news events on TV, I see the same look on their faces that I used to see on my father's face when he went to vote: a look that says, "I'm part of this great country and nobody's going to keep us down."

On September 11, we found out that you don't have to know people personally to feel their pain and anguish. I once heard a priest say that our job in this life is to keep each other warm. September

11 was a horrible wake-up call for us to do just that. Now I see people doing it all the time. Ethnic origin has faded into the background because we're all Americans—Americans, keeping each other warm.

ART GARFUNKEL

Art Garfunkel is a musician.

Perhaps if I steal from Thomas Wolfe and give him his proper due—not the "man in full" but the "homeward angel"—he might reappear for you.

Then see him up there where the Rockies rise, his legs dangling over the ledge above Denver, eight thousand feet in the air. Before him the plains, behind him the Pacific, stars coming out on a summer night, and everywhere the twilight falls on America.

To the right is Amarillo. Beyond it the Astros at play; over my shoulder Seattle, over the other, beyond the great Canyon, gas fumes and fast food mix with the smell of L.A. Hear the blues parade across the stage—up from New Orleans into Chicago—see all the clusters of light beyond. Follow the fashion of rock 'n' roll: St. Louis to Cleveland to Philly to bond the nation's soul with music in its ears.

And in our hearts, love of the physical entity, America. Identity in doubt. We can't go home again, so we're runaway vagabonds lost in twilight wondering what we're about.

LEEZA GIBBONS

Leeza Gibbons is executive consulting managing editor and host of the daily newsmagazine Extra.

I was pouring orange juice into glasses when I saw the horror and instinctively, the nurturing side of me knew to say, "Kids, why don't you go upstairs and get dressed first, we'll have breakfast in a little bit." I wanted to shield them from the traumatic images. Even though time stood still, the day marched on. We continued with our morning almost to serve as a denial that anything so awful could be happening. It was only in the car on the drive to school that the walls came tumbling down for me and my children broke the silence when they saw me wiping back tears as I got into the carpool lane.

"What's wrong, Mommy?"

I said, "Everything's gonna be okay, sweetie, it's just that our world changed today and I'm sad about that."

It was the end of the innocence for us as a nation, and for our children, who in that unspoken moment had to trade in what should be their birthright of a carefree childhood for a more cautious and protected view.

Going to school that day was the only normal part of their routine. It gave our children a sense of comfort, and when they got home we started a conversation, a dialogue that is ongoing. We gathered together and prayed for the families whose lives have been shattered, for the soul of New York, which was so sick with unthinkable sadness, and we offered up our own prayer of gratitude. I was pitifully unprepared for the questions that came: "Why do they hate us so much?" "What if the plane runs into our school?" "Were the passengers wearing their seat belts?" I knew that it was such a pivotal moment, perhaps a defining moment globally and intimately for our small family of five.

We Americans have no interest in being victims, and as President Bush outlined our military's plan of action, our family went into action as well. To help them process their emotion, we painted tiles, each child with their own thoughts through an interpretation of the image. My four-year-old painted an airplane, for my ten-year-old it was the Twin Towers with the fires raging, and my twelve-year-old daughter painted an American flag with the words that we saw emblazoned everywhere: Never Forget.

After a church service to honor the victims and pray for wisdom for our leaders, we planted what the kids call a "freedom tree" right outside their bedroom windows where they could see it grow. As we piled dirt over the roots, we talked about the things that will grow from this unconscionable event: patriotic pride, families appreciating the freedoms we hold dear, compassion, respect for our heroes. And just as the tree grows stronger every day, so will our nation. They put a stone at the foot of the tree that simply said, "9–11–01, we will never forget."

Our field resources at *Extra* were of course dedicated to covering the remarkable stories that emerged, the overwhelming grief, the search for the bodies, the nonstop funerals. But my personal window was open to the stories of the children, and I began to seek interviews from parents, psychologists, and mostly from the kids themselves. One night my son asked me, "Mom, have they found Osama bin Laden?" "No, not yet," I said. "If he asks for forgiveness before he dies, will he go to heaven?" he asked. "Because I don't think I ever want to see him there."

By now it seems as if we have dissected every aspect of this story. Our nation has been fed around the clock with morsels of coverage that for a time seemed to fall short of satisfying our horrendous appetite. But while I think we're still pounding our chests with pride, and I know we're cautiously moving through our daily lives, as time passes another aspect of our national character is emerging. We want answers and we need to figure out where the truth is. We are the people who questioned the authenticity of our mission to the moon, the people who wonder about UFOs and alien sightings and Area 51. We're a nation that feels lied to about the Kennedy assassination, and it is that nation of people, regular folks who are not powered by any organization, who will insist that while we fight the war on terror that we also understand what's at its core so that we can have answers for our children.

NIKKI GIOVANNI

Nikki Giovanni is a poet and the recipient of the Langston Hughes Award for Distinguished Contributions to Arts and Letters.

My America

Not a bad country . . . neither the best nor the worse . . . just a place we call home . . . and we open that door . . . to the tired and the poor . . . to the huddled masses yearning . . . to be free . . . to those in need . . . because we need . . . to be needed

Not a bad country . . . but adolescently indifferent . . . with time running out . . . on our innocence

Not a bad country . . . but attention must be paid . . . to how the bounty came to be ours . . . to all the people . . . who make up the people . . . that we are

A thought here and there . . . a "maybe this could have been done differently" . . . the patience that is required of those who aspire to be . . . if not the best . . . then at least better

Not a bad country in fact . . . most likely . . . the best possible hope . . . of human beings . . . to exemplify differences that: can share prosperity . . . can tolerate choices . . . can respect individuals . . . can teach us all . . . to love

MARVIN J. GIROUARD

*Marvin J. Girouard is chairman and CEO of
Pier 1 Imports, and a board member of
the United States Fund for UNICEF.*

AMERICA: A LOVE AFFAIR

I don't think you can love your country without
experiencing all of the layers of complexity that you
find in any important relationship. When we are in
love, we treasure the simple joys and grow to appreciate the deeper blessings. As the relationship
matures, we step up to embrace the responsibilities
and challenges.

Even when I was young, I understood I couldn't
take from Lady Liberty without giving back. I loved
her too much, and she had given me so much in
return. Some of the simple joys I treasured were
country-and-western music, Mickey Mantle in the
bottom of the ninth inning, barbecue sandwiches and
cold beer on hot summer days, Texas A&M and
Dallas Cowboys football games, and Elvis's blue
suede shoes. She made it possible for guys like me to
marry a Texas girl from my hometown area and stay
happily married for thirty-five years and honor God
according to my own beliefs.

America has also given me the opportunity to
stand tall in cowboy boots and in combat boots. To
protect her and our way of life, I joined the navy
and fought in Vietnam. Many of the people I served
with in the military felt the same desire I did after

September 11. We wanted to join the young men and women who signed up for the armed services after the attack on New York and Washington, knowing full well we probably couldn't pass the physical! I'm proud to see that the younger generation still has people willing to pay the ultimate price, if necessary, to defend our country and its citizens.

Protecting Americans involves more than guarding them against foreign enemies. It also demands supporting those in need everywhere. Disease, poverty, and illiteracy are just as destructive to our way of life. Personally, as well as through Pier 1 Imports, the great corporation I am privileged to lead, I support organizations including UNICEF, the Susan G. Komen Breast Cancer Foundation, the United Way, and our local public schools. Americans show their patriotism by helping others through hard times. The outpouring of support for the victims of September 11, not only those in our country but also the women and children of Afghanistan, proved that.

Pop psychologists agree that for relationships to survive, people need to communicate. Voting is my chance to be heard. Democracy depends on participation. I'm not interested in any other form of government, so I always make it to the polls. It is my greatest wish that our children and grandchildren live life to the fullest in the freedom of America—the land that I love!

JOHN GLENN

John Glenn is a former NASA astronaut and was the first American to orbit the earth. He served as a United States senator from Ohio.

More than any other place in this world, America means opportunity. Our unique Constitution provides not only protection for each individual but also freedom of opportunity to become whatever his or her dreams and talents can lead to.

But along the way, Americans are people who make democracy work by respecting one another. They are honest and fair with their neighbors and they honor the laws made by their elected representatives. They reach out to help those in need, and pitch in to provide schools and services in their communities.

Responsible Americans inform themselves about the natural, political, and social worlds in which they live, and they take part in politics—from which come the people who represent us all in working to make the Constitution a reality. They show their commitment to democratic processes by running for public office or serving on decision-making boards, councils, and commissions at all levels of government.

True Americans consistently speak out against inequality, injustice, and bigotry, and they value individual freedom of conscience. They are respectful of our flag and staunch in defense of the United States Constitution and Bill of Rights. Most of all, Americans are ever faithful to the timeless ideals of liberty and justice for all—the liberty of opportunity, and the justice of equality.

Freedom *from*—

Freedom *to*—

Andrew J. Goodpaster

General Andrew J. Goodpaster (USA-Ret.) commanded the Eighth Infantry Division and was director of the Joint Staff, commander of the National War College, deputy commander of U.S. forces in Vietnam, and the commander of NATO forces. He is the author of For the Common Defense, *and his numerous honors include the U.S. Medal of Freedom.*

The special meaning of our country to its people is to be found, I firmly believe, in the rich gifts of individual freedom, opportunity, and well-being that our citizens enjoy.

Those gifts are based in great part, of course, on the vast physical resources of our land itself, developed through the enterprise, the industry, and the commerce of generations past and present. But they derive even more from the ties that bind us together as a nation and a society—a society shaped by its dedication to the highest principles of human endeavor: respect for the dignity of the individual, for the arts and sciences of civilization, for learning in all its forms, and most notably for the rights enshrined in our Constitution's Bill of Rights, and in its government "of the people, by the people, and for the people." Our country is inspired by its history of courage and sacrifice in gaining our independence, in preserving its Union, in defending itself and its allies when attacked or threatened with attack.

It is a country that seeks, over time, always to do better, to right past wrongs, to protect its people, to honor commitment to its service, and to keep the way open for each of us to "be all you can be."

OTTO GRAHAM

Otto Graham played professional football for the Cleveland Browns, leading the team to seven league titles in ten years. He was the NFL's Most Valuable Player in 1953 and 1955, and was elected to the College and Pro Football Halls of Fame.

I was a sophomore basketball player at Northwestern University in 1941 and it was my twentieth birthday. Still nursing bruises from the football season, I was given the night off so I could attend the Wildcat gridiron banquet. Recruited as a freshman off an undefeated frat house team, my biggest varsity thrill was throwing two touchdown passes to beat Ohio State and rookie head coach Paul Brown. I would receive some nice birthday honors that night but my first basketball game was days away and I would rather have been at practice.

The guest of honor was Gene Tunney, the former heavyweight champ. Dressed in navy whites, Tunney was the director of President Roosevelt's Naval Physical Fitness Council. Expecting to hear boxing stories or related sports anecdotes at the evening finale, the audience was instead assailed with a discourse on Japanese aggression; a real concern, but not a popular subject on a festive night. After first fidgeting, the crowd began to murmur, heckle, and boo, forcing Tunney to regroup. After his words were drowned out once again, the frustrated champ voiced his disappointment at his generation's youth before glumly taking his seat.

That was the day before one which would live in infamy and my last as a collegian in a country not at war. The morning after Tunney was driven off the dais, the Japanese Empire attacked Pearl Harbor. It was a birthday I would never forget, and suddenly basketball wasn't that important anymore.

I've thought often of that day and how much it changed my life. I remember how my eyes were freshly opened to the things that made America great and how easily we can take it all for granted. I thought of the diverse backgrounds of my teammates and how well we meshed when chasing a shared elusive dream. I thought of the tolerance Americans usually celebrate and how it slightly strayed that night. And I thought of the freedoms that allowed Tunney to have his say in the first place. I realized that America isn't easy and we don't always get it right. It's only important that we try.

Until 9/11, I thought that younger generations would never understand. As I celebrated my eighty years with my children, grandchildren, and great-grandkids a few months later, I realized I was wrong. Diversity, tolerance, and an uncompromising thirst for freedom are very much alive and well in my family and in our nation. As long as we embrace the resolve, pride, and unity we shared the morning after those two horrific events, the American dream will surely outlive us all. Dream well.

GORDON A. HAALAND

Dr. Gordon A. Haaland is president of Gettysburg College in Gettysburg, Pennsylvania. He is on the twenty-member steering committee of the America Reads program and is a member of the board of the American Council on Education. He is a founding board member of the Council on Higher Education Accreditation and also serves on the board of the Eisenhower World Affairs Institute.

My America is a personal story, and it is about opportunity.

I remember well my immigrant parents trying to make sure that my siblings and I spoke English correctly and knew how to read effectively. English was not their first language but they viewed the proper use of language as a tribute to their adopted country. This country gave them the opportunity to find good jobs, buy a house, and raise a family. Their success enabled them to help family back in Norway right after World War II, when we had numerous relatives come stay with us in the U.S. while they tried to make new lives here.

The most important opportunity this country provided, in the minds of my parents, was education. My father came over as a young man, having gone to sea at age fourteen. He spent his life here as a seaman who never had the opportunity to go to college because he could not afford it. My father was both proud and envious of the college opportunities of his children.

More than any other country, America provides a breadth of opportunity for students to pursue an education. Our citizens can pursue learning through certificate, two-year, four-year, and graduate and professional programs in liberal arts colleges and universities, technical schools, business schools, and many other types of institutions as well as in virtual schools. One can study almost any discipline or subject area known in the modern or ancient world. Substantial financial assistance is available through private, state, and federal grants, as well as loans and work-study. No other nation combines the broad incentives with the encouragement we provide for our citizens to pursue a higher education. There are no national limits on spaces in schools or colleges.

What are the consequences? Recent studies continue to demonstrate that the more education a person has, the more likely he or she is to be both financially and personally successful, regardless of race, ethnicity, or other personal attributes. More importantly, the very democracy that provides us our freedoms and opportunities is dependent on an enlightened and educated citizenry.

What does my country mean to me? It is the nation where hundreds of thousands of people came to start a new life—to have the freedom to learn. My parents came to this country as one of these many to provide their children with the opportunity to get as much education as they could so that their grandchildren could attend the finest colleges and universities in the country. America was my parents' opportunity. The education it permitted was mine.

ALEXANDER M. HAIG JR.

General Alexander M. Haig Jr. (USA-Ret.) is the former secretary of state, NATO commander, and White House chief of staff.

The heinously tragic events of September 11, 2001, once again confirmed the historic American tendency to withstand a high threshold of pain. The terrorist acts in New York City, in the skies of Pennsylvania, and at the Pentagon aroused the "sleeping giant" within each of us. "Patriotism" has once again become a popular word that tends to express our unity whether in adversity or in victory.

But truly what is this phenomenon called "patriotism"? As I have often said, patriotism has always been an expression of one's willingness to dedicate a certain portion of oneself, one's talents and energies, to something beyond oneself. To adopt unto oneself the basic values that have made our nation what it is, and to be willing to struggle—and if necessary, to fight—for those values.

From across this great land individuals have demonstrated their commitment to the values that have made our nation great. From all walks of life, patriots have stepped forward, giving of their time, talent, and resources to affirm that that for which the United States of America stands shall forever be a beacon of hope for peoples around the world. The land of the free, the home of the brave rings even truer since September 11, 2001.

PETE HAMILL

Pete Hamill is a journalist and best-selling author.

One August night when I was a boy, I heard my father weeping in the dark. He was an immigrant from the bleak bigotries of Northern Ireland, and when he was twenty-seven he had lost a leg to gangrene, playing soccer in the immigrant leagues of Brooklyn. That loss did not keep him from work. He worked as a clerk in a grocery chain, in a war plant in Bush Terminal making bombsights, and as an electrical wirer in a factory in Brooklyn. He married my mother, also an immigrant from the north of Ireland, and fathered seven children, of whom I was the oldest.

On this scalding summer night he wasn't weeping because the family, as always, was short of money. He wasn't weeping out of self-pity, that most unforgivable of sins. He was weeping in sheer physical pain. The stump of his ruined leg was covered with blisters caused by the heat wave. In the factory where he worked, there were concrete floors and no air-conditioning. The pain was more than he could bear. My mother rose in the dark and whispered to him and placed ice on the blistered stump, and consoled him and nursed him until he was quiet. In the morning, he went to work.

He went to work because he was now an American and this country allowed him to work. He wasn't asked about his religion. He wasn't asked about his family history. He wasn't asked about his political beliefs. This was America.

I'm sure he wasn't alone. All over New York a half-century ago, all over this nation, there were men like him, and women like my mother. In spite of pain, they were thrilled to be in a country where they could work. They were thrilled to be in a country where they need bow before no king, where they could choose their leaders, where they could join trade unions, where they could read any book from the shelves of the public libraries. Their lives were far from perfect; many died poor, most worked at jobs they did not like, too many were subjected to ignorant bigotries. A few became criminals. A few were broken by America, and went home in defeat.

But the overwhelming majority had a belief in the day after tomorrow. Tomorrow might not be better for them, but the day after surely would be wonderful. They lived to see their American children become the first in all the centuries of their families to graduate from universities. They saw their American children find work in places where their bodies were not blistered by summer heat. Some of their children became mayors or senators. Some triumphed in art or the academy, in journalism or business, in sports or entertainment. All made the United States a better country.

For me, the presence of those immigrants is fundamental to this nation. A century ago, their hope, idealism, and capacity for work shaped the armature of the modern American nation. And that is as true today as it was before World War I, as a new generation of immigrants adds its presence to the United States. I see them each morning on the streets of New York. That Chinese woman laboring on Canal Street is my mother too, working for her children. That Mexican man heaving garbage cans into a truck at two in the morning: he's my father. They are part of the alloy that gives this nation so much strength. They help account for our tolerance, our liberal freedoms, our generosity. They enrich us in many other ways too: with labor, with music, with food, with humor, with their fundamental dignity.

Some Americans might be stirred into love of country by the sight of B-52 vapor trails. I prefer the image of a young Mexican-American woman in cap and gown, surrounded by weeping parents and aunts and uncles and brothers and sisters, walking into an early summer afternoon, clutching a diploma. In that moment, she honors her family. She honors mine too, and all those where a parent once wept in the dark. Above all, she honors America.

BARRY HANTMAN

Barry Hantman is a teacher in New York City.

America means that the Old World with its rigid and royal ways has been embraced by the New World of opportunity and hope. America is a chance to undo hateful patterns.

Anastasia is one of the best students I've encountered during my teaching career. A vibrant young lady with blond hair and blue eyes, Anastasia hails from Minsk, the largest city in the former Soviet republic of Belarus. My grandmother fled a Jewish *shtetl* near Minsk. Avoiding pogroms and the czar's secret police were worthy Russian Jewish goals a century ago. Grandma Lena would never see her parents again when she immigrated to New York City. The jam-packed Lower East Side awaited. What were her thoughts as she sailed past the Mother of Exiles in New York Harbor?

It's now been eighty-five years since my grandmother's exodus. On a class trip to the United Nations, I look through a grimy window to catch a glimpse of Lady Liberty. Later in the morning, Anastasia can be seen glued to a corner of the gift shop. She is drawn to some colorful UN stamps. "Are you a collector?" I inquire. "I used to have a large stamp collection but we left everything behind when we quickly departed." I discreetly purchase the stamps and hand them to Anastasia as a surprise gift. "Now you must begin another collection!" She smiles and agrees, "Yes, it's important to start over."

A few weeks later, Anastasia asks me to write a letter of recommendation for her college application. The historical irony does not escape me. Grandma Lena's Jewish grandson is helping Anastasia succeed thousands of miles from the same Dnieper River that flows through both our families. In Minsk at another time, Anastasia and I would have harbored many negative preconceptions about each other. But in America, "We have it in our power to begin the world over again" (Thomas Paine).

CHARLES B. HARMON

Charles B. "Chuck" Harmon broke the Cincinnati Reds' color barrier in 1954 by becoming their first player of color. He also played for the St. Louis Cardinals, the Philadelphia Phillies, and the winter leagues in Puerto Rico. He has worked with the First Appellate District Court of Appeals in Cincinnati, Ohio, as an administrative assistant for the past twenty-five years.

My feelings about living in the United States of America can be summarized in one word: *Great!*

Being free to live, work, and raise a family is what makes this country great. Why do we need a catastrophe to awaken us from our dilemmas, to be kind, thoughtful, loving, considerate, and sympathetic to one another? Does our self-centeredness blind us to our surroundings and limit our minds to superficial things?

Thousands of immigrants flock to this great land every day, some legally and some illegally, but all seeking a new way of life. Even people who criticize the United States rarely try to escape this peace-loving land to go elsewhere. Nevertheless, many Americans take what we have for granted. I think that being an American should not be taken for granted, and that it imposes on each of us an obligation of endurance and tolerance. We need to reach out and embrace each other and the people of other countries and to work harder to understand and communicate with each other. Only then can we learn that we have much in common, that we want many of the same things for our families and for our countries.

Growing up in the United States was one of the luckiest things to happen to me. Being black or being poor can be a big obstacle in life. But how I approached these obstacles and dealt with them helped me to develop common sense and a way to solve problems that has sustained me throughout my life.

Being the tenth of twelve children in my family meant that I was always at the bottom of the list. It was difficult for my parents, Sherman and Rosa Harmon, to raise a family that large through the difficult times of the 1920s and 1930s. But both of my parents had taught school early in life, and they made sure that each of us graduated from high school and saw nine of us attend college. With the help of God and the church, my parents created strong bonds among the members of our family. It is a tribute to my parents that those bonds remain strong to this day.

With my country, I have lived through a lot of changes, including the stock market crash, the Great Depression, the Japanese attack on Pearl Harbor, the Second World War (during which I served in the navy), the conflicts in Korea and Vietnam (through which my wife, Daurel, and I raised our three children), and, most recently, the September 11 terrorist attacks on the World Trade Center and the Pentagon. I am concerned when I hear that U.S. citizens have sold out our country by disclosing to other governments our confidential secrets, or that our own government has endangered its people by disclosing too much information or by ignoring the threat posed by the presence in this country of people of questionable character.

But looking back over my lifetime, I am confident in our country's ability to endure any emergency. Throughout its history, the United States has remained a free nation. I am very proud and honored to call myself an American and to have been able to raise my family in this great country of ours, just as my parents did.

My life has taught me the importance of self-respect and respect for others. Everyone wants to get ahead in this world, but those efforts may fail. Most people do not plan to fail, but they fail to plan. Thus, I have learned to plan ahead and map out different situations to guide me in the direction that best suits my ideas and me. But I have also learned to diversify, so that, no matter what obstacle presents itself, I can at least avert a major disaster. And I have learned to be flexible, to adjust and be adaptable to changes. Finally, experience has taught me to help others less fortunate than myself.

I believe that we, as citizens of this country, owe it to our country to abide by its rules. If we could live our lives by a strict code of personal and public ethics, the whole world would profit with dignity, humility, and a sense of purpose. There would be less bloodshed and more peace and harmony in the world.

Through the years, growing up in a small town in the Midwest, playing high school and college basketball, serving my country in the navy during World War II, playing the grand old game of baseball in (and a role in the integration of) the major leagues, I have met people from all walks of life. It has been an experience beyond my wildest dreams. *Only in America—thank God!*

PAUL HARVEY

Paul Harvey is a radio legend.

It's testing time again.

Every generation has been tested.

On this rebellious planet storms are part of the normal climate.

Sometimes the storm involves economic chaos— or a prolonged drought; sometimes internal civil strife; sometimes a military confrontation.

We face a new testing time every lifetime.

Some of us have been professional observers of several lifetimes. We remember epidemic TB, the crash of '29, the Dust Bowl, Hitler's holocaust, Dien Bien Phu, and Saddam Hussein. We resent challenges but are no longer panicked by them.

During each test some Americans feared our country was going to hell. It did not.

It went through a little hell but it came out of the crucible heat-tempered and stronger than before.

Now we are intimidated by the Taliban. Osama bin Laden epitomizes for this generation what we called "hippies" or "flower children" in the last generation.

These antiestablishment, unwashed counterculture rich kids have hijacked Islam for their personal aggrandizement.

Where the previous generation of student radicals

identified with "peace," the Taliban's seminarian spoiled brats espouse holy war. A parallel perversion of a worthy purpose.

So—Americans—we've been there, done that.

A few wars ago our anxiety focused on the hideous force of the unharnessed atom.

Now, in retrospect, we can see that the A-bomb was a disguised blessing.

We Americans are outnumbered by potential enemies seven to one. War with bayonets we could not win. The big bomb was the equalizer that cut the limitless hordes of Asia down to our size.

Now we can see that an all-wise Almighty entrusted this hideous instrument to our tiny fraction of the planet's population—first—not for our destruction but for our deliverance.

Times do not change. Time goes in circles.

The atom bomb altered the strategy of warfare but we are never without war for long.

In the three and a half thousand years of recorded history, fewer than 8 percent of those years have been warless.

It has not been 150 years since we Americans were at war with ourselves.

So storms are a part of this planet's normal climate.

An eternity is being prepared somewhere. A perfect place. We have to demonstrate here whether we deserve to be there, and if there were perpetual sunshine there would be no victory.

So it's testing time again. And from everything I have seen since 9/11 we are passing the test again and with our colors flying.

TONY HILLERMAN

Tony Hillerman is a mystery and suspense writer whose works focus on the Navajo Nation. His Seldom Disappointed: A Memoir *was published in 2001.*

September 11 caught my wife and me near the Canadian border, a thousand miles from Albuquerque. That gave us a fine opportunity to observe how midwesterners at assorted airports and hotels reacted to news of the attack. We saw shock and anger then, and a good measure of concern and sympathy.

In my travels since then I've noticed that anger hasn't subsided. But I am proud and happy (but not at all surprised) to report that the only evidence of fear I have seen has been in Washington, D.C., with the reaction of congressmen and federal officials to the poison-pen anthrax letters. These key people in our government were terrified into making fools of themselves, into abandoning their jobs, shutting down their offices, and behaving exactly as the terrorists must have hoped.

I asked my Albuquerque pharmacist what he thought of the national television campaign to terrorize America about anthrax. "Well," said he, "we always have some sheep and cattle people getting that stuff. A couple of fatal cases in Mora County. But let's put it in context. We have five dead of anthrax this year, and over a hundred thousand dead of pneumonia, and thousands killed by staph and other bacteria. I'll do my worrying about those."

I am sure that what little public fear was produced among Americans in those first weeks after the attack was primarily the product of the mass media selling it, and the endless "the sky is falling" warnings cabinet members were delivering. But Americans aren't easy to scare. I'm an elderly fellow with memories of Pearl Harbor, of the rush to recruiting offices, of getting myself blown up by the Germans in that cold winter of 1944–45. But I have no memories of Americans afraid—even then when there was a legitimate reason for fear.

After months of unscientific research, I can report that Americans know the only hope the terrorists have of destroying the freedom we love is if our terrified lawmakers and the White House folks manage to take away—and think we are scared enough to let them rob us of—our rights to free speech, privacy, and the equal justice of our criminal code.

We won't let that happen.

JOHN HOEVEN

John Hoeven is governor of the state of North Dakota.

American history presents some jarring milestones, a handful of major events when the American people are stunned into action and reflection over an incident so unconscionable as to enlist our moral and political resolve. September 11, 2001, was such a milestone.

As we have before, however, our nation rose to the occasion with resolve and purpose. We did so, not with vindictiveness, but with a healthy sense of who we are: a people bound in our determination by unity, strength, and tolerance. September 11 and our response to it prompted me to think about the vast differences between Americans and those who have declared a war on the freest and most generous nation that history has ever seen. And those differences are stark and telling.

Whereas Americans prize diversity, the al-Qaeda and Taliban enforced prejudice against women, foreigners, and those who hold a faith different from their own; whereas Americans value freedom of expression, under the al-Qaeda and the Taliban, the presses ground to a halt, and the airwaves fell silent; whereas Americans value peace and showed forbearance and patience, even when our embassies and citizens were attacked around the world, our enemies shunned dialogue and pushed away the peace table; whereas Americans prize life, and painstakingly avoided civilian casualties in the recent conflict, our enemies explicitly targeted and continue to target the innocent as a matter of policy.

America, to me, is a refuge not only for those who seek freedom from political and economic oppression around the world, but also a refuge for an idea: the still young notion that people can and should live together in freedom and harmony. *E pluribus unum*— out of the many, the one. That is what accounts for our resilience and our resolve in the aftermath of September 11. That is an idea worth fighting for.

JAYNE HOWARD-FELDMAN

Reverend Jayne Howard-Feldman is founder of Be an Angel Day and Inspire Your Heart with Art Day. She is also curator of The Light at the Top of the Stairs Healing Arts Center and the author of Commune with the Angels.

ANGELS AMONG US

In 1993 I began promoting Be an Angel Day, celebrated annually on August 22. It is a nonprofit event to raise people's awareness about being of service to others. I believe there are angels among us, as stated in Hebrews 13:2: "Be not forgetful to entertain strangers: for thereby some have entertained angels unawares."

Up until 9/11, I was unaware of a certain legion of angels in our midst. They weren't wearing wings but rather the uniforms of the New York City fire and police departments. On September 11, 2001, I watched firemen and policemen answer the ultimate call of service—laying down their lives to rescue as many lives as possible. I was humbled by the greatness of their service when I saw a video of firemen going into the south tower of the World Trade Center. As I watched this video several months after 9/11, I knew these brave individuals had been photographed going into the "valley of the shadow of death." These brave souls did not fear death, for they eternally embody the light of service. I believe that even though they closed their eyes to earth and opened them to heaven, they in some way continue to serve. It was in their blood here on earth; it's in their spirit in heaven.

In looking at anagrams from the word AMER-ICA, I observed the words: I AM RACE. I asked myself, "What race of beings would define the diversity of our population into one nation?" After 9/11 I answered my own question from what I learned from the firemen and policemen who died helping others. I am an American. I am a member of the Grace Race. God's grace was shed upon our nation. It wasn't delivered by a member of the heavenly host from a celestial realm. God's grace was shed upon us by the firemen and policemen who shed their blood and lives for others. God bless them and the members of their brotherhood across America, a brotherhood whose members continue to serve as earth angels. Yes, there are angels among us. I say a prayer of thanks to God every day for them.

MIKE HUCKABEE

Mike Huckabee is governor of the state of Arkansas.

Three days after the terrorist attacks of September 11, 2001, I was driving past a public high school. Three words on the school message board caught my attention. Had those words been displayed a week earlier, they might have provoked a lawsuit. No lawsuit now, but perhaps a lump in the throat. The simple words expressed the sentiments of so many: "God bless America."

A day earlier, the youngest of my three children, who is a sophomore in college, had called to talk about her feelings. She was discovering a new sense of patriotism and appreciation for our country. For the first time in her life, her freedom was threatened. She was beginning to realize God had, in fact, blessed America, and in doing so had blessed her and all Americans.

Our uniqueness is in our spirituality. It's not something on which we can all agree, but there's an unapologetic recognition of the role and significance of providence in our history, law, culture, and preservation. We had grown almost afraid to acknowledge it. But during a national tragedy, public figures from all walks of life and all faiths were openly calling for people to pray.

JANICE HUFF

Janice Huff is a meteorologist with WNBC-TV New York.

September 11, 2001 . . . I began the day with my usual ritual. I awoke around 8:15, searched through the sheets for the ever-elusive remote, and turned on the television to catch the weather report (I am a meteorologist, weather is my business). The big news of the day was the mayoral primary here in New York City, and my colleagues at WNBC were discussing the candidates and their platforms. Then came a familiar sight, the view from the sky camera atop 30 Rockefeller Plaza, providing a spectacular view of the Empire State Building and the twin towers of the World Trade Center. The sky was hazy, but clear, and 80-degree temperatures were expected later that afternoon. What a perfect day this is going to be! I thought to myself. But who would have thought the unthinkable: that in less than thirty minutes from that moment, my view of the twin towers would be changed forever. As I sat perched on the edge of my bed, I gazed at the dark, smoldering, gaping hole in Tower One. I watched in disbelief as the second plane came into frame at the top of my TV screen, and headed straight for Tower Two. I sat speechless as the news came from Washington and Pennsylvania of more terror in the sky, and I wept as the towers, filled with innocent lives, came crashing down to earth. . . .

Even though I didn't lose a loved one in the collapse of the twin towers, I feel as if I have lost my mother all over again—I am overcome with grief every time I look at the spot where they once stood. The sadness is sometimes overwhelming. But just as in the loss of a loved one, I know I must move forward; we must move forward; America must move forward. And we will be stronger because of all that has happened. On September 11, 2001, the best in America came forth. On that day, we were able, as a people, to step outside of ourselves and bring the good to the surface for all the world to see. From this day forward we must stand together as one nation against all evil, united under one flag to let freedom ring forever.

JON M. HUNTSMAN

Jon M. Huntsman, who served as special assistant to the president and as White House staff secretary under President Nixon, is chairman of the board of the Huntsman Cancer Institute at the University of Utah and international chairman for the American Red Cross.

The founding of the United States of America was one of history's most unlikely achievements. That an ill-equipped, woefully outnumbered army had the audacity to challenge the mighty British Empire was incredible, yet valiant forces, united in the battle for independence, albeit with some outside assistance, prevailed.

The history of America is sprinkled with events that defy reason and remind us of our precious legacy: the Boston Tea Party, Valley Forge, the Declaration of Independence, the Constitution, Gettysburg, the Emancipation Proclamation, the Alamo, Pearl Harbor, D-Day, Iwo Jima, Desert Storm, and now New York's World Trade Center.

Some would have us believe that divine providence had nothing to do with either the founding of our nation or its survival of seemingly overwhelming challenges over the years. There is evidence, however, that the opposite is true. History records that America's mighty leaders humbly acknowledged the divine mission to which they pledged their lives, fortunes, and sacred honor.

George Washington, in his first inaugural address, said, "No people can be bound to acknowledge and adore the invincible hand, which conducts the affairs of man, more than the people of the United States. Every step by which they have advanced to the character of an independent nation seems to have been distinguished by some token of providential agency."

Thomas Jefferson, author of the Declaration of Independence; James Madison, sometimes called the Father of the Constitution; and Benjamin Franklin (to name a few), one of our greatest patriots, echoed General Washington's views. Franklin stated, "If a sparrow cannot fall to the ground without His notice, is it probable that an empire can rise without His aid? I believe without His concurring aid we shall succeed in this political building no better than the building of Babel."

May God continue to bless and guide this great nation, and may our fellow citizens acknowledge His hand in all things and strive to be worthy of His watchcare.

JANIS IAN

Janis Ian is a folksinger and songwriter.

MY GRANDMOTHER'S COAT

My grandmother's mother came to her with a well-lined coat and told her to hide it from the Cossacks. So she did.

My grandmother's father came to her with a few gold coins and told her to hide them from the Cossacks. So she did.

My grandmother's sister came to her and told her to sew the coins into the lining of the coat and hide it from the Cossacks. So she did.

Then my grandmother went to *her* grandmother and said, "Why did they buy the coat? Why did they buy the coins? Why did I sew them into the lining?"

And her grandmother said, "You are a Jew. If you ever have to flee this country because of it, you will need something to bargain with during your journey." And one day, she did.

My grandmother came to me and said, "Take the lining from this coat. Take the coins from the lining. We are safe now." So I did.

We came to America so I would not have to wear that coat.

BIL KEANE

Bil Keane is the creator of "The Family Circus"
comic strip.

Since my fifty-year career in cartooning has centered around family life, I look at all the people in our nation as family. Of course, some are like that ne'er-do-well Uncle Charley, or a greedy cousin Louise, but most are loving, cordial, decent people of all races and ethnic backgrounds.

I look at the recent wave of patriotism as an

increased affection for each other that we all share and are willing to show. The flag is a beautiful symbol of unity and pride that binds us together. The playing of "The Star-Spangled Banner" brings tears to my eyes and it should.

The national family structure has changed through the years in many ways. However, it is still our most important haven for comfort.

Home and family are indeed the heart and backbone of America.

FRANK KEATING

Frank Keating is governor of the state of Oklahoma.

AMERICA: ONE NATION AT LAST

Like most Americans, Oklahomans watched the events of September 11, 2001, unfold with shock and horror. But uniquely among our neighbors from the other forty-nine states, we had been there before. The terror bombing in Oklahoma City on April 19, 1995, left an indelible mark on our state and community. It also taught us some valuable lessons the rest of America learned on September 11.

First among those lessons was a truth brought home by the eyewitness images from both 1995 and 2001: We really are one people. When terror strikes, when neighbors need help, we shed the artificial hyphens that once seemed to divide us and go to work for the common good.

I remember Oklahoma City's ground zero in those first hours of April 19, 1995. The stretcher brigades coming out of the rubble pile included white Oklahomans, black Oklahomans, Oklahomans with red and with yellow skin, men and women, professionals and volunteers. Six years later, we saw the same scenes from New York and Washington—Americans helping Americans, with no regard for the classifications that were supposed to have divided us.

We've heard a great deal in recent years about those so-called divisions. Some political leaders have even sought to pit group against group. For a time it seemed that everyone wanted a hyphen, that it wasn't enough to simply be an American. Oklahoma City changed that for us; now, September 11 has changed it for the rest of the nation.

The fundamental lesson of those two dates, when America was attacked by terror, is that hyphens and arbitrary dividing lines no longer mattered.

Not long after the attacks of September 11, I visited one of my state's largest military installations. Some of the soldiers there were training for possible deployment overseas in the battle against terrorism—and all of them were eager and willing to go. I was struck once again by the togetherness I saw, the shared mission and the devotion to country. The only color those soldiers saw—and they were from every possible racial and ethnic background—was army green. The flag they saluted was red and white and blue.

Diversity is our nation's strength, not, as some would have had us believe before September 11, our Achilles' heel; real diversity is a white American, a black American, a red American, and a yellow American each hoisting one corner of a stretcher, or lining up to donate blood, or forming an infantry squad to defend our land. Diversity is no longer a barrier; it's a bridge, linking us all together.

KITTY KELLEY

Kitty Kelley is the author of numerous books including His Way, *her unauthorized biography of Frank Sinatra.*

For a millisecond, the billows of smoke from the World Trade Center looked soft and fluffy, almost benign. But then we saw the bodies rain down as human beings hurled themselves from windows to certain death below. We couldn't smell or taste the acrid choke of burning rubber and melting steel but we saw various survivors stagger out of that inferno, vomiting, gagging, and gasping for air.

The searing scene, replayed over and over for the next few days, immobilized me. Uplifted by the valor of New York's policemen and firemen and rescue workers, I felt guilty, yet grateful, that I had been spared. I also felt limp with helplessness because there was nothing I could do. Gripped by all sorts of fears, I wobbled around in a world suddenly turned upside down. Days of nausea followed nightmares. Then I received a bouquet from a friend in London, which opened my heart. Between those flowers and some inspiring words I began to find my way back to blue skies.

The flowers were red, white, and blue. Tied with a perky patriotic ribbon, they looked like they'd been plucked from a victory garden. The simple card said: "By way of solidarity." The thoughtfulness of that unexpected gesture made me feel the warmth of strong arms across the sea. The bouquet filled my house with color, fragrance, and the wartime spirit of Winston Churchill.

The words came from William Faulkner in 1950 when he accepted the Nobel prize for literature. He talked about the ability of the human spirit to endure despite the fear of being blown to smithereens. He said he refused to accept the end of man:

It is easy enough to say that man is immortal simply because he will endure: that when the last ding-dong of doom has clanged and faded from the last worthless rock hanging tideless in the last red and dying evening, that even then there will still be one more sound: that of his puny inexhaustible voice, still talking. I refuse to accept this. I believe that man will not merely endure; he will prevail. He is immortal, not because he alone among creatures has an inexhaustible voice, but because he has a soul, a spirit capable of compassion and sacrifice and endurance.

I read those words over and over until I could watch the burning towers on television without crying. When my solidarity flowers died, I made a bow of the red, white, and blue ribbon, and wore it proudly every day. Yet even salved by flowers, ribbons, and words, I still couldn't make sense of the terrorism. But I did recover my belief in love and hope and honor and community. Most importantly, I remembered the enduring power of each of us to prevail.

CORETTA SCOTT KING

Coretta Scott King is the widow of civil rights activist Dr. Martin Luther King Jr. She has continued her husband's mission through her work as founding president, chair, and CEO of the Martin Luther King Jr. Center for Nonviolent Social Change in Atlanta, Georgia.

As we commemorate the first anniversary of the atrocities of September 11, we Americans are called to provide for the world an inspiring example of goodwill toward people of all races, religions, and nations.

As the most diverse nation, America must set an indelible example of multicultural unity and inclusiveness for the benefit of humankind. Our country is not so much a melting pot as a vibrant mosaic of diverse people and groups. We must affirm the sisterhood and brotherhood of all people—every race, every ethnic and linguistic group, every religion, women and men, gay and lesbian, people with disabilities—everyone. Every group and every individual has something important to contribute to our society, and our strength will forever be rooted in our remarkable diversity.

I believe we were all tossed together on these shores to fulfill the ancient human longing for unity. America is the diversity laboratory of the earth. We have been chosen to show the world how good life can be when diverse peoples come together in a spirit of brotherly and sisterly love and work together for the common good.

Let us vow that September 11 will only strengthen the bonds of solidarity between all of America's races, religions, and cultures. Let us use this national tragedy to reach out to one another with greater openness and love, to put aside the animosities that have divided us across man-made barriers for so long.

There is much truth in the old saying that "living well is the best revenge." But let's give the phrase "living well" a new, deeper meaning—not living well in the material sense, although we certainly want America's remarkable prosperity to thrive and expand. Instead, let's "live well" by becoming more loving, more caring and compassionate, more generous and open-hearted to people in need, not only in our own country, but around the world. If we can do this, then we will honor the precious lives that were lost on September 11 and the sacrifices of all who have suffered as a result of this tragedy in the most meaningful possible way.

HOWARD KISSEL

Howard Kissel is a theater critic and columnist for the New York Daily News.

Some years ago a descendant of Mark Twain reminisced with me about the day that he, as a child, accompanied his forebear to Oxford to receive an honorary doctorate. The other honorees that day included Rudyard Kipling and Camille Saint-Saëns, who were received warmly, but when Twain stepped forward the attendees hurled their tasseled caps into the air and cheered.

The reason the story moved me when I first heard it is because, in my naïveté, I had always imagined that America was perceived with the same enthusiasm and affection as one of its most beloved authors. This illusion had been punctured before but never as profoundly as on September 11.

Yes, I know our foreign policy has not always been as enlightened as it might have been. I also know that even in our attempts at benevolence we have often blundered. But what other power that has as mighty an army as we have has not used it for conquest?

We are the product of the Enlightenment. The revolution that began in 1776 is the only one that genuinely succeeded. (The jury is still out on the consequences of 1789, which, with the Terror that followed, unfortunately provided the model for most subsequent revolutions.) Our institutions, which have served us so miraculously for over two hundred years, are based on Reason, and our national pride is not merely an expression of boastfulness about our history but a faith in the universal principles we represent.

The assault on the twin towers was an attack on Reason itself, the mathematical disciplines that made such glistening structures possible and the intellectual framework underlying our bountiful and uncommonly civil and generous society.

By the time I left for work that brilliantly sunny morning I knew the towers had been hit, but I did not see the TV images of them falling until later in the day. I first heard about it on the bus on my way to the office. A man near the back of the bus was describing it from what someone was telling him on a cell phone. It seemed—and still seems—totally absurd.

His incredulous voice blended with the high-pitched twang of a frizzy red-haired tourist in a short-sleeved white blouse, a black vest bedecked with rhinestone pins, and denim shorts jabbering to her friend, "Didn't Bush pull out of some conference or something?"—as if the U.S. withdrawal from the UN-sponsored harangues on racism in Durban the week before justified what was happening. (One needn't travel to the Middle East to see the limited inroads Reason has made over the centuries.)

This juxtaposition of an unimaginable calamity

and a response of such dizzying inanity might have amused Mark Twain. But the whole thing is darker than his world allowed. The monologue in which Huck Finn wrestles with his conscience over the "evil" of freeing the slave Jim is a scathing indictment of the institutionalized racism of his day.

Twain believed in a world where common sense would triumph. Could he have imagined a time when all-consuming hatred would trump Reason?

I am glad that my memories of that horrendous day include something funny. Laughter at least brings the inconceivable into the realm of the comprehensible. Something characteristically American is that one of our great literary figures is a humorist. Laughter is a form of affirmation, a kind of faith that what we see is not all there is.

Rebecca Kolls

Rebecca Kolls is gardening and lifestyles contributor for Good Morning America *and host of the nationally syndicated* Rebecca's Garden.

The tragedy of September 11 affected me like millions of others. But I witnessed a bigger effect experienced by my two children.

Five generations of my family have chosen the United States as their home—a safe haven. The first generation came to this new land fleeing controversy with hopes to find a secure place in a land called America. And now, more than a hundred years later, the fifth generation fears and questions the security that beckoned their ancestors. I saw it firsthand with my young children. No one will forget that fateful day, September 11, 2001, especially the children. The day the world changed. The day America changed forever. "Land of the free and the home of the brave." Simple words we often take for granted. Words that now have a new meaning. What is it to be free? My nine-year-old daughter can tell you. The 9/11 tragedy taught her and my son valuable lessons they couldn't learn in school. Watching the jets crash into the twin towers was not some thriller movie. This was the real thing. It was hard for them to understand. "Can they find us here, Mom?" A spine-chilling question. And for the first time I had no answer. It was bad enough that my home was threatened. But seeing how it troubled my children and how I could only offer a hand and hug hit me hard. This was real. Night after night my twelve-year-old son, the courageous big brother, slept in our room to quell the nightmares of people falling from the windows. Visions of attacks interrupted my daughter's sleep—"No, they can't get us here," I finally said, feeling a gut-wrenching twist that "Oh God, please let me be right."

For the first time in their young lives, the evening news was more important than a game of hockey or a good book. Night after night they watched. They wanted answers, and shared the horrible grief that gripped America. A couple days after the attack my daughter and I were out gardening. It was an especially quiet day. The skies were silent. Then, suddenly, we heard a jet engine moaning in the distance. She immediately looked into the sky and quickly moved to my side. I, too, felt something eerily amiss. In a short while, we saw the noise. An airline jet flanked with F-16s. "It's okay, Madison," I said with tears in my eyes and anger in my heart. "These are good guys. They will protect us." She looked up at me and smiled. The days that followed continued to teach my children about the cruel world around them. They saw the horrible atrocities in Afghanistan, including the injustices against women. They now know what it means to be free and why it's a privilege to live in America. And more than anything else, they are proud of their

American heritage. Everything they've learned in school, from the Declaration of Independence to civil rights to women's suffrage, seems to make better sense now. This is what we cherish in America.

The loss of life, security, and freedom because of that fateful day was a terrible loss indeed. But, what it did to my children perhaps will help them grow into leaders looking for ways to guarantee a safe home for the generations to follow. With a hint of naïveté, my son boldly told my husband and me, "I can't wait until I'm old enough to fight for my country." Profound words from a new generation. America, "land of the free and the home of the brave," *will* live on.

MICHAEL KORDA

Michael Korda is editor in chief at Simon & Schuster.

The attack of September 11, 2001, should bring home to all Americans two vital points. The first is that America's foreign policy is and ought to be a primary concern of ours, and that foreign policy is not just a matter of making trade agreements or exchanging ceremonial visits. The countries of the world have *not* necessarily been brought closer to each other or made more friendly toward the United States by trade, television, the Internet, or even self-interest, and deep gaps of cultural differences, political and religious beliefs, traditions, ambitions, and national interests still divide us and can explode into dangerous crises. The end of the Cold War has not made the world into the Peaceable Kingdom, and Americans should be prepared to follow and support America's national interests, where necessary, with force, particularly when they involve conflict with those who do not accept our most cherished and central beliefs, including a pluralistic society, religious freedom, gender equality, the rule of law, and all those things which are represented by the Anglo-American common heritage of the Magna Carta, Common Law, and those principles that led to the drafting of the Declaration of Independence, the Constitution, and the Bill of

Rights. We have an obligation to face the fact that our heritage of freedom has to be defended in every generation, that from time to time we will have to make sacrifices for that heritage, and that not every country or culture accepts or admires what that heritage means.

Second, the attack should remind us that Jefferson's great phrase in the Declaration of Independence, "the pursuit of happiness," is something we must always keep in mind. Our country represents a great experiment. The notions that "all men are created equal" and that "the pursuit of happiness" is a vital object of government are still not true in most of the world, or even understood in many parts of it. It is our privilege to pursue that happiness, both in our private and our public life, and to do our share toward building that "city on a hill" the Puritan settlers dreamed of, but we must constantly remind ourselves that more is involved than self-indulgence or gathering wealth or watching MTV or driving a new SUV. Happiness, as Jefferson defined it, involves a government committed to the freedom of the individual, and citizens pursuing a more perfect and just society. It is, in fact, a long, difficult, and demanding process, which we have been pursuing, with ups and downs, for over two hundred years, and which, by its very nature, challenges all those, all over the world, who seek security in the past, or in trying to prevent change, or in trying to restrict and restrain the freedom of others; and from time to time those challenges will be violent, and will call upon the same spirit that signers of the Declaration of Independence showed when they took on Great Britain at a moment when she was the world's dominant superpower—the willingness to risk our lives for our principles.

GUNTA KRASTS-VOUTYRAS

Gunta Krasts-Voutyras is an immigrant from Latvia and a textile artist.

A very, very long time ago, in another time, another culture, another country, I received a care package. All the other elementary school children in my class did too. I, however, had a photograph in my package: a picture of the little girl, my age, who had packed this gift. I no longer remember what wonderful goodies were in this delight from Heaven but I do remember the photograph: a girl, my age, about twelve years, sitting on the bottom step of her porch. She had long, beautifully curled hair and a marvelous dress. Everything surrounding her looked so clean and well taken care of, the shrubs, the path leading from the sidewalk up to the house. She was looking into the camera and smiling.

For a child who had endured detention camps, cold water cascading onto her emaciated body in mass shower rooms, had her hair "shampooed" with gasoline, been yelled at and pushed around by armed guards, this photo was surely of a place in Heaven.

In due time, I, together with my family, immigrated to the United States. Late in the evening in spring of 1949, the SS *Laplanda* dropped anchor outside Boston Harbor. Several hundred of us, the former refugees, stood around on deck in a combined feeling of anxiety and fascination. The lights of Boston seemed dreamlike, like a Christmas gift wrapped in sparkling paper. Most of us, young and old, stayed up all night, milling about, fantasizing, worrying about how it would be. Will our parents find a job? What kind of job? How will we learn English? Who will teach us? What about school? To get good grades one needs to understand the teacher's instructions. A very worrying point.

All this imminent new life we were all embarking upon became more spirited as the ship slowly chugged into port. We disembarked into a huge terminal. Long tables placed end to end stood across the width of the great hall. Each table above it had a letter from the alphabet. We understood this type of processing; we had been through this dozens of times before. The difference was that this particular one was taking place on the soil of the free world. Therefore, we knew, once we walked out the door, we were truly in America and free.

To record all the strange names took hours. My feet hurt, only because each of my shoes was from a different pair and two different sizes, neither of which fit, one too small and the other too big.

On the outer perimeters of the terminal I noticed some very gracious ladies standing by tables laden with boxes of something edible. At closer look the boxes contained something round and fluffy looking. These ladies were exquisitely dressed in bright colors of green, blue, red, and pink, and all had on their arm a white band with a red cross on it. They had beautiful shoes and stockings, and their hair looked like they never slept on it.

These women were walking around offering these things from the boxes to the former refugees. I noticed when someone took one of these round things, their fingers got white powder on them.

I could see the disapproving look in my grandmother's eyes; she had brought me up to never accept anything from a stranger and definitely never, ever eat in public.

Being the willful, independent child I had always been, I took a round thing from the box as the lady came by. It melted in my mouth, white sugar flying all over my face. And strangely, it had a hole in the middle.

This was my first introduction to American generosity and kindness, and I can never pass a display of white sugared doughnuts without remembering that day in March of 1949.

To be an American is an incredible privilege. This means pride in my country as I present my American passport at an airport check-in. This means intellectual freedom. This means ability to obtain an education. This means freedom from persecution, the privilege to own property, to speak up when a wrong is done without fear of being shot. This also means religious freedom by having the privilege to worship in the church of one's choice. My America means walking on a street without being accosted with a demand for ID. It means freely buying food in a store.

This is *my America*. This is where my family came to for *freedom*. I hold my America in the greatest respect and will never, ever allow anyone to hurt this nation.

RICHARD D. LAMM

Richard D. Lamm, former governor of the state of Colorado, is director of the Center for Public Policy and Contemporary Issues at the University of Denver.

A great philosopher once said, "We define the world by the questions we ask." Thank you, Hugh Downs, for focusing us on the essential question of what America means to Americans. If we forget to ask ourselves what America, freedom, and democracy mean and how important these are to our lives, we are halfway to losing our national heritage.

Too many Americans believe that God is an American who will watch over us no matter how hedonistic, selfish, myopic, or self-absorbed we become. This is a dangerous hubris. No great nation in history has ever withstood the ravages of time. Greatness is not a guarantee, it is a continuing challenge. Toynbee warns us that all great nations rise and all fall, and that the "autopsy of history is that all great nations commit suicide."

To me America means that caring, farsighted, and patriotic people can form a "more perfect union" that allows people the freedom and opportunity to explore and develop their talents no matter what those talents may be. America is the guarantee of self-government; it is the continual search for justice and fairness; it is dedication to a system of social mobility that allows anyone to rise above the circumstances of birth.

America developed what Tocqueville called "habits of the heart." America, better than any previous nation, developed meaningful citizens. Citizens do more than share a zip code; they have multiple things they do or honor in common: voting, volunteering, donating blood, attending town meetings, trusting their neighbors and coworkers. They have a civic pride and are committed to a substantial degree of "civic engagement." Citizens have some common loyalties. James Fallows puts it this way: "In the long run, a society's strength depends on the way that ordinary people voluntarily behave."

A great nation needs its citizens to feel they have a shared stake in the future. It needs a shared language, shared culture, shared norms and values. It needs, in short, social glue that is the essence of nationhood. It must understand that all members to a certain degree have a shared fate. To say my fate is not tied to your fate is like saying, "Your end of the boat is sinking."

Greatness is not a guarantee, it is a continuing challenge. It must be won anew each generation. It is now our turn to preserve and perfect these principles for those who follow.

FRANCES LANGFORD

Frances Langford is a singer, actress, and entertainer. She appeared in several films and joined Bob Hope in entertaining World War II troops in the United States and abroad.

When Hugh first asked me to give a brief statement on what my country means to me personally, I pondered this big subject with a sense of awesomeness. I had thoughts of so many things to share in light of recent events on September 11 and considering all I have seen and done in my own life. I will try to put into words my heartfelt beliefs and how they relate to this wonderful country we call home—the United States of America.

I love the U.S.A. and the spirit of this country that is reflected by the American people. That fortitude is represented in many different ways, but I am especially interested in, drawn to, and appreciative of our courageous military men and women. To believe in America means to believe in freedom, peace, equality, and justice—among many other attributes. To deem these certain aspects of decency important enough to fight for and possibly die for is the ultimate service and can only aid in the continued promise of these American ideals. That is why I chose to serve our young soldiers during World War II, along with Bob Hope and many others, in the best way I knew how—entertainment! Looking into the eyes of our young GIs and singing to them before they headed off to battle, visiting wounded soldiers in makeshift hospitals, and just trying to bring some smiles from home to our boys was one of the greatest honors and the greatest sadnesses for me—it was truly bittersweet. I was so drawn to help in some way for the cause of freedom because I love this country and everything we represent.

My America and what my country means to me can be summed up by something a true American once said about this country: "In all it is a great country. It's the best and the worst one I ever lived in, and I been living in countries for fifty-four years next November fourth" (Will Rogers).

Sure, we have a lot of problems in the good ole U.S. of A. You must take the bad with the good, constantly working on the ills of society to make an even better America. The bottom line for me is that we live in the greatest country on earth.

ANTHONY LEWIS

Anthony Lewis is an author and former New York Times *columnist.*

In 1783, after the Revolutionary War but before the Constitution had knitted the American states together, Massachusetts had a convention to write a constitution for itself. John Adams did the drafting, and he came up with a phrase that I think is this country's great contribution to the philosophy of government. We want, he said, "a government of laws, not men."

The words are a bit hackneyed by now, but their meaning has not lost its power. For two centuries the idea of reliance on law distinguished the United States from other countries. They relied on the skill of leaders, or suffered from their leaders' folly. For Americans the ultimate answer was always to be found in law—especially our fundamental law, the Constitution.

We forget now, most of us, how novel was the idea of binding a country to a set of written rules. Only those rules, I believe, could have held together this vast nation, with all its differences of culture and ethnic background and region. Only once has the system broken down: when the South broke the constitutional compact in the Civil War.

Today we take it all for granted. When a president breaks the rules, he can be called to account as

Richard Nixon was. No one is above the law. That, for me, is what makes America special. Without that assurance, that safety, all of this country's wealth and power would not make it—to copy Shakespeare—the envy of less happier lands.

Since World War II, other countries have copied the American system and adopted written constitutions: countries as different as South Africa, Germany, France, Hungary. Those constitutions, too, have the crucial provision of enforcement by courts.

In times of stress and war, America has departed from the protections written in our Constitution. In 1798, worried about the terror in revolutionary France, Congress made it a crime to criticize the president. During the Civil War, Lincoln suspended *habeas corpus*. In World War II the government moved Japanese Americans from their homes on the West Coast to camps in the desert. But in time we regretted those abuses and apologized for them.

Since September 11, 2001, we have been in another time of stress. Again, constitutional guarantees have been overridden. But I have faith that our tradition—our commitment to law—will prevail.

Joseph Lieberman

Joseph Lieberman is a United States senator from Connecticut and a former vice-presidential candidate.

America is the greatest experiment in the history of civilizations, a nation intended to be ruled by the will of the majority and protect the rights of the minority. Our founders didn't just create a country for themselves to govern; they built the framework of a nation resilient enough to withstand changing times, flexible enough to absorb internal diversity, and strong enough to fight external threats. Few societies of such ambitious design have achieved their objective—but we have, and have grown more and more successful as our citizenry has grown more diverse in race, religion, ethnicity, and background.

That's because, for all its unique capabilities, the United States is ultimately guided by its conscience. We have the mightiest military the world has ever known, but we use it with prudence for principles. We have the strongest and most vibrant private sector in the world, but work to focus the power of our markets on raising up all of our people. We prohibit state establishment of religion, but celebrate individual faith and give it a place at the national table. We are confident, but our pride and patriotism never eclipse a healthy instinct to scrutinize our own actions and hold our own government to the highest standards. We are made up of almost 300 million voices from all across the world, the most diverse human community ever assembled, but in times of crisis, we are capable of speaking with a resoundingly clear and consistent voice.

This is a great nation, imperfect—as any human creation must be—but striving always to safeguard the rights to life, liberty, and the pursuit of happiness that our Declaration of Independence makes clear are given by God to every individual. Our country was the first to declare that those rights precede any government, any law, or any ideology, and it will never stop fighting to protect and preserve the precious values that are our birthright and those of people all over the world.

ART LINKLETTER

Art Linkletter is an Emmy and Grammy Award–winning television and radio personality and author of the best-selling Kids Say the Darndest Things.

Like many other American citizens, I am originally a "foreigner." Since my birthplace was Canada, I suppose I could qualify as a "semiforeigner." Nevertheless, on September 11, 2001, we were all searingly welded together by the catastrophe at the World Trade Center. It was like a call to arms!

Unlike any event since Pearl Harbor, this unmitigated horror unified the nation and precipitated the stunning declaration of "war on terrorists" the world over. It left behind it a kaleidoscopic vision of a horrified and saddened America. Many were personally traumatized by the loss of dear ones. Others were frightened, panic-stricken, and wondering who would be next.

Economically, a nation struggling with a recession was struck a damaging blow—especially the travel industry, hotels, and resorts.

But the flip side of this painful record reveals a return to a former time when we were a more sensitive, helpful population. The friendly attitude, the more courteous reaction to trifling annoyances, and the general feeling of partners instead of competitors brought back memories of life in the forties and fifties as I recall them.

As a professional lecturer, I fly an average of 200,000 miles a year speaking at some seventy meetings in churches, colleges, town halls, and business conventions. Everywhere I go since 9/11, I sense a quick and almost automatic burst of applause when my comments touch on the "mission" of America. When I talk about our freedoms, our opportunities, and the wide horizons of life in the U.S.A., the response is like touching an electric switch.

Traveling is a vexatious and tedious task. Security measures tax the patience of almost everyone. But, surprisingly, I see less of the traditional American impatience. I see few "flying fingers" from young people in traffic jams. And I sense a new appreciation of brotherhood.

I hope and pray we maintain this friendly way of life long after terror is vanquished!

DICK LOCHER

Dick Locher is a Pulitzer Prize–winning editorial cartoonist for the Chicago Tribune.

ANNE GRAHAM LOTZ

Anne Graham Lotz is president and executive director of AnGeL Ministries, a nonprofit organization offering Christian outreach. She is the daughter of Billy and Ruth Graham.

On September 11, I watched my television screen in horror as the twin towers of the World Trade Center not only erupted into raging fireballs following the jetliners' impact, but then imploded. It was incomprehensible that buildings that took seven years to build, which had steel beams running every thirty-six inches from the basements to the 110th floors, could disintegrate so quickly into a six-story-high pile of dust, ashes, and debris. Amazingly, when the dust settled after the implosion, we were told the foundations of the building were intact.

Those buildings in many ways represent America. Our nation has many voices that speak with different accents. We come in all shapes, sizes, colors, and creeds. Yet in our diversity we have unity because we share the same foundation of faith in God. This foundation is described in our pledge of allegiance as "One nation under God." It is identified on our currency with the phrase "In God We Trust." And as our nation has figuratively dropped to its knees in prayer following 9/11, it is increasingly evident that after the dust of shock, fear, and anger has settled, we are still standing firm on our foundation of faith!

The twin towers also represent us as individual Americans. We seem to be strong and prosperous, but in truth many of us are unable to withstand the sudden impact and intense heat of disaster, disease, divorce, depression, death, and other difficulties. Upon impact, we have the choice of whether or not we will stand firm on a foundation of faith in God, or whether we will implode in fear, anger, prejudice, hate, and unbelief. In the weary days ahead, as we adjust to living under the daily threat of terrorism and at a time of war against it, it is my earnest prayer that we will shore up the foundation on which we are building our lives.

I have chosen to build my life on the firm foundation of faith in God, who personally understands suffering and what it feels like to have someone you love die a horrible, untimely death. Because God loved you and me so much, He gave His only Son to die on the Cross to be our Savior. And He promised that when we place our faith in Him, we will never perish, but have eternal life. God gave us His own Son that we might have peace in our hearts for today as well as hope in the face of death for tomorrow.

May God bless America—right down to her foundation!

FRANK G. MANCUSO

Frank G. Mancuso is chairman and CEO of Metro-Goldwyn-Mayer and MGM/UA Home Entertainment.

I have had the opportunity to live the American dream, starting as an usher in a theater in my native Buffalo, New York, to become chairman and CEO of two of Hollywood's most famed studios, Paramount Pictures and later Metro-Goldwyn-Mayer. Because of that most fulfilling experience, America has been clearly defined for me as the land of incomparable opportunities to be pursued by anyone to the extent that their talents, abilities, and energy will take them. The pursuit of any opportunity in this great country has been undertaken with full and complete knowledge of the security that our government provides us as citizens, both in the laws of the land and the protection of its armed forces. Those assurances have allowed Americans to pursue their dreams and ambitions with determination and a clear focus, without being distracted by concerns of safety and security. That has been a given as part of our birthright in this nation of nations.

As chance would have it, I was in New York on September 11, having traveled from Los Angeles and arriving in Manhattan on September 9. In the midst of the horror of the events of that day, I witnessed a public that was in a state of shock, not believing what their eyes were seeing—this was not possible in this city, in this country. But it was possible and it was true. I also witnessed something else, when the realization of what had taken place had sunk in, and the indomitable spirit of Americans took over. Not only in New Yorkers who were at the scene of the tragedy, but also in their brothers and sisters across our country, who that day all became New Yorkers. That unified determination to protect our country, to bring to justice those who committed this horrible act and to defend us from future acts, is all part of the greatness of this country. A land that creates so many opportunities for its inhabitants to live a complete and full life of happiness and fulfillment instills a pride, a love for the values of that land. It is normally a quiet feeling, deeply felt but not too often expressed. Tragic events in history like the Pearl Harbor attack and the World Trade Center disasters have awakened and stirred those feelings into a cry of a nation . . . "Not on our land."

The strength of this nation comes from the sense of fairness of its citizens. Doing what is right is an important part of the American tradition. Standing up for a just cause has been the American way. Seeing those causes through tough and difficult times is part of the American grit. We have overcome much since September 11. We have awakened with a new determination—a new sense of unity. We stand as one, more so than I can recall in a long time. In the end it is all about how much America means to us.

AL MARTINO

Al Martino is a singer whose career took off with the 1952 record "Here in My Heart." Other hits include "I Love You Because" and "Spanish Eyes."

My deep feelings of patriotism started long before September 11, 2001. They started in the year 1943 when, as an underage sixteen-year-old boy, I joined the United States Navy. Seeing the flag being raised over the still smoldering Pentagon during those dark September days brought back a flood of memories.

February 22, 1945, while serving my country on Iwo Jima, I watched another flag being raised on Mount Sarabachi by six brave marines. Three of the six marines were killed in the days afterward. It never occurred to me at the time that I might also die for my country. It never occurred to the victims of September 11, either.

What was most incredible about the events of September 11 was not only the destruction, but also how Americans responded. I was so proud of our country's many, many heroes. I also remembered fighting side by side with the heroes who lost their lives fighting for our precious freedom during World War II. We, as a nation, have remained resilient to protect and preserve our liberty and independence to anyone who might threaten it.

As the Stars and Stripes went up on a remote Pacific island a half century ago and as they now fly over an embassy halfway around the world in Kabul, I realize that our flag and the country for which it is a symbol are not mere ideals for which our nation stands. Our nation is a living, breathing embodiment of these dreams. What other country since the beginning of recorded history has fed their vanquished enemies and rebuilt their infrastructures and economies without asking to be repaid? It is not hyperbole to say that America is the greatest nation on earth. It is a simple fact whose profundity somehow got overlooked. Not anymore, thanks to the spirit of the people of the United States of America!

PETER MAX

*Peter Max is an artist. He designed the
United Nations series of stamps.*

A noted physicist, Gerhard Staghun, once wrote,
"Our own sun, relative to Earth, is a gigantic thermal power plant; but relative to our galaxy, the
Milky Way, it is a tiny luminous point of medium
brightness that would be hard to find in the outer
arms of the spiral. And this point of light is orbited
by a tiny blue speck, hundreds of thousands times
smaller, on which a very strange species roams as of
late, regarding itself as very big and important."

On this tiny blue speck of dust where this human
species roams, many great lands flourish. And there
is one land in particular, called America, that is
most special. For it is the land where the brave pioneers from all other lands have settled, and now call
home.

America is a quilt sewn together with the threads
of freedom, democracy, compassion, and creativity.
It is the melting pot where I can stand outside my
Manhattan studio and see almost every race of
every nation walk by within an hour. It is the most
creative and generous place on the planet.

In these times of extraordinary challenges, we
must always remember what makes America so
magnificent—its people, the creative thinkers, the
pioneers. We are the birthplace of some of the

greatest movements of our times: democracy, civil rights, woman's equality, ecology, and animal protection. As an artist I see creativity all around me: the incredible wonders of technology, medicine, and art. We are the most creative place on this little blue dot. In this country you can achieve anything.

We live in a universe that is more than 15 billion years old. And, as Carl Sagan put it, "If the fifteen-billion-year lifetime of the universe was compressed into one year, dinosaurs would emerge on Christmas Eve; flowers would arise on December 28th; and men and women would originate at 10:30 P.M. on New Year's Eve. All of recorded history would take place in the last ten seconds of December 31st." In this case the life span of America is but half a second long.

America today is the threshold of a unified and peaceful world. I think we've come a long way.

THEODORE E. MCCARRICK

Cardinal Theodore E. McCarrick is the archbishop of Washington, D.C.

WHERE DO WE GO FROM HERE?

The smoke has finally cleared away and the persistent fires are no longer burning. It was not the smoke that brought the tears to our eyes, nor the fires that moved our hearts to fear. It was the awesome, terrible loss of people we love, of neighbors we knew, of colleagues with whom we worked, the tragedy of lives never finished, of pain and suffering never imagined.

We wonder about tomorrow. Will our nation change? Will it be a time of fear? Will the awful experiences of 9/11 turn our hearts to hatred and revenge?

This must not be. All that is foreign to the ideals and values of America. We must come back to that motto on which we built this great nation more than two hundred years ago. We must never forget that it is "in God we trust."

All our religions teach us the sanctity and dignity of human life. They all teach us to love God and each other. They do not—and cannot—teach us to hate, or teach us to destroy, or teach us to kill the innocent.

This then must be our resolve for tomorrow. This must be the journey on which we all embark together. We will build up our trust in each other, we will teach our children that generosity is better than riches; that love of neighbor is better than power; that care of the poor and the downtrodden and the victims of injustice is the greatest of all pursuits and the one that pleases God the most.

It will not be easy. Those who hurt us must be brought to justice. Those who seek to destroy us must be made to realize that it is a dangerous and impossible adventure. But these lessons we will teach within the boundaries of our system of law and according to the precepts of our values.

We do trust in God as a people and as a nation. We know that He loves us and that He will see us through these dark days. We will overcome even this crisis. We have placed our hope in the Living God.

COLMAN McCARTHY

Colman McCarthy directs the Center for Teaching Peace in Washington, D.C. A former Washington Post *columnist, he is the author of six books on social justice, including* I'd Rather Teach Peace.

AMERICA AND SOME GREAT NUMBERS

- In 2002, Congress gave $334 billion to the Department of Defense, which is about $900 million a day, or $11,000 per second, or more than $2,000 from each taxpayer.
- Nine hundred million dollars a day is four times greater than the Peace Corps budget for a year.
- The U.S. military budget is twenty-three times larger than the combined military budgets of the seven nations alleged to be threats to America.
- Every day that U.S. military programs are given $900 million, some forty thousand children, according to Oxfam, die from hunger-related or preventable diseases.
- An estimated five thousand cluster bombs dropped by U.S. pilots on Afghanistan in the fall of 2001 remain unexploded.
- On average, forty thousand people a month die in the world's fifty-nine wars or conflicts. According to the Center for Defense Information, 80 percent of them are fought with U.S.-made weapons. American companies are the world-leading seller of ammunition, for an arsenal of more than 500 million small arms and light weapons.

- Food banks and homeless shelters in major American cities report as much as 25 percent increases in calls for help from poor people.
- On February 5, 2002, the day that military increases were called for in the new federal budget, four homeless people froze to death on streets within miles of the U.S. Capitol.
- More than seven hundred people on the nation's death rows have been either gassed, shot, drugged, hanged, or electrocuted to death since 1977.
- Thirteen retarded people have been executed.
- Ninety-nine death-row prisoners have been freed by exonerating evidence.
- America imprisons more people than any country in the world.

Thirty-five years have passed since Martin Luther King Jr. said, "I am convinced that if we are to get on the right side of the world revolution, we as a nation must undergo a radical revolution of values. . . . We still have a choice today: nonviolent coexistence or violent coannihilation."

MIKE MCCURRY

Mike McCurry is chairman and CEO of Grassroots Enterprise, Inc. and served as press secretary to President Bill Clinton.

There is no better way to see America than to criss-cross the country with those who would seek to lead us as our president. I have had that opportunity more than several times, working in national political campaigns. America is the greatest formula ever invented to resolve differences between people who might not otherwise see eye to eye. Every four years, we set aside our particular interests and figure out what we share in common, even as we argue and debate. I think we are rather like those big balls of string that we collected as kids—lots of pieces, long and short, colored and not, frayed at the edges or holding together pretty well. There is no glue that keeps us wrapped closely together, only the bond that comes from sticking together side by side. Drawing on the various kinetic energies of each other, we roll along as one America; *E pluribus unum.*

JAYNE MEADOWS

Jayne Meadows is an Emmy Award–winning actress.

A CHILDHOOD MEMORY FROM JAYNE MEADOWS

The bomb tore open our home in WuChang, China, and landed on the dining room table but never exploded. From upstairs, I challenged my sister, Audrey, to a spitting contest: who could spit the farthest through the gaping hole in the floor and hit the bomb below without falling into the dining room. Neither of us won—our missionary mother caught us just in time, thank God. She was, of course, frantic since my older brothers had been entertaining themselves by digging bullets from the walls of our father's church.

Mother was at least comforted by the fact that a stray bullet from a Communist soldier had obliterated only one face in her favorite painting of *The Last Supper*—that of Judas Iscariot.

We escaped that night on a Yangtze riverboat built to hold a hundred passengers. There were almost five hundred of us fleeing to Shanghai, which was teeming with other foreigners all seeking passage out of this war-torn land.

Our family of six was assigned two unheated rooms in a rat-infested warehouse filled with filthy furniture on which we slept, ate, and passed the days awaiting safe passage to America.

Many months later, our ocean liner glided through the "shining sea" of New York Harbor past the welcoming "Lady." Mother rushed us up to the main deck and with tears of joy streaming down her face, said, "Oh, children, look—this is America. Your new home." I'm crying now recalling that magic moment.

God bless America, land that I love.

Howard M. Metzenbaum

Howard M. Metzenbaum is a former United States senator from the state of Ohio. He created the Sun Newspapers chain in the 1960s and now serves as chairman of the board of the Consumer Federation of America.

This country of ours is one incredible place. It has been called more than once the land of great opportunity, but, in my mind, that is the understatement of the year. My family had great difficulty in meeting the challenges of the Depression. I will never forget the day I went down to get into my old used car. It was gone. My dad had sold it for fifteen dollars to make a payment on the second mortgage on our home. We still lost the home to foreclosure.

From that shaky financial beginning, I have been able to lead a successful business and legal career, serve as a United States senator, and watch my children and grandchildren grow and thrive. The open society of this country—its commitment to opportunity, to justice and education for everyone, and its compassion—made it possible for me and many others like me to start with nothing and rise to positions of leadership.

We are a country that welcomes immigrants seeking a better life or fleeing injustice. We are a country where anyone can rise to sit on the Supreme Court, run a major corporation, or teach our children. We are a country with enormous freedom where people can openly voice their opinions and organize to advance them. We are a country where people can freely choose the life they want to live.

We must fight to protect these opportunities for everyone, and this has been an important part of my life. Early in my career, I filed lawsuits to open up several local private facilities operating on public property. We won the cases and opened the facilities to people of all races and religions. I can remember fighting to reopen schools closed for years to avoid desegregation and deny black children an education. These positions did not always make me popular, but the people in this country are broad-minded and tolerant enough to support those who take unpopular positions, sometimes contrary to community views. America does not make conformity a standard for choosing political leaders.

America is a country like no other. We did not build our government upon the roots of a nationality that already existed, or upon a hereditary aristocracy with the right to rule others. Instead, we built our country on a simple but powerful idea that extends opportunity and compassion to all—all people are created equal and share the right to "life, liberty, and the pursuit of happiness." It is an idea we must always cherish and protect.

KATE MULGREW

Kate Mulgrew is an actress known for her portrayal of Captain Kathryn Janeway on the television series Star Trek: Voyager.

Strange, how suddenly the tides of fortune and well-being can change and the skyline of one of the world's greatest cities be muted. This nation can be likened to a superb athlete, young and vital, unsurpassed in strength and skill. What a profound shock to see the runner stumble—and fall. And all around this hero America watches, incredulous—brought quite abruptly to a condition of vulnerability both foreign and completely disarming.

It is my personal conviction that a tragedy of this nature acts as a unifying force—but beyond that, and more important, such devastation affects the getting of wisdom. From wisdom, empathy is born. We are now able to view our nation, and one another, with clarity and compassion. The dangerous notion of invincibility has been dispelled and in its place the far greater virtue of compassion, which enables us to walk hand in hand not only with one another but with all people who have suffered the malignancies and horrors of amorphous evil.

Fear is not necessarily the worst by-product of this kind of terror—fear is the natural, primitive response to pain. Certainly, there is an inexpressible agony in the breaking of a nation's heart—but there is an evil more legion than that practiced upon us should we allow our spirit to be broken.

This must not happen–nor will it. The long-distance runner must keep his eye on the race; only now he will take courage from the competitor at his side and acknowledge that ultimate truth: We have always been in this race together. That is the glory, and the reward.

JOHN J. NANCE

John J. Nance is aviation analyst for ABC News and a novelist.

There was a moment in the maturing hours of September 11 when countless human minds on this small planet we share looked figuratively toward Washington and New York and wondered what was to become of us, this flagship nation of the modern world.

But while the outpouring of concern from most quarters for the most generous country in human history was appropriate and heartwarming, ultimately there was one pivotal element in the equation that was in no danger whatsoever: the *spirit* of America, a unique, indispensable, and indestructible force of hope and faith.

The United States is a living ideal, a nation uniquely dedicated to life and propelled by an indefatigable optimism that there is both meaning and mission to this existence. America is a strong and driven cross-section of the most determined humans on earth, the sons and daughters of people who have struggled through Darwinian odds to come to this continent and build a better life in the exhilarating atmosphere of freedom, an environment rich in the oxygen of human confidence and accomplishment, a nation continuously renewed by our very diversity of ethnicity and intellect.

Our forefathers and mothers for so many generations have proven our national worth through our deeds and our resilience. It was, after all, the United States that vanquished a previous evil known as the Axis, then saved and rebuilt the nations who had caused the world such agony. It is always America in the forefront of any effort to spread humanitarian aid and political stability, human rights and the benefits of freedom, regardless of the costs. And it has always been the province of Americans as people to suspend our family arguments during a time of crisis and come together with a common purpose and a common determination that knows no insurmountable barrier.

It is with such immense power of purpose that we once again rise to the challenge, this time to defeat an evil idea, a philosophy devoid of real connection, with religion that holds that this life is meaningless and disposable, a repugnant vortex of pessimism.

What attacked America was a distillation of the wrong that those brilliant few in Philadelphia were fighting in 1776 when they bet their honor and their lives on the principle that there is a brighter purpose to life. And we shall continue to be the steward of that ideal for all of mankind.

PATRICIA NEAL

Patricia Neal is an Oscar-winning actress.

I am a survivor. On February 17, 1965, after a series of devastating strokes, several papers around the country ran obituary notices for me. But Tennessee hillbillies don't conk that easy. In the weeks, months, and years that followed, I learned to think again, I learned to walk again, I learned to talk again. I literally reconstructed my life. In doing so, I have been surprised and delighted by the number of people who have told me over the years that my recovery was an inspiration to them.

I feel a great affinity with those whose lives have been so tragically altered by the events of September 11, 2001. In that one stroke of fate all those lives have been changed forever; grieving men and women have lost their life partners, grieving parents have lost their children, and perhaps most tragically, grieving children have lost their parents. As all of these thousands of men and women, boys and girls, struggle with their anger and grief and loss, my heart goes out to them. As they reconstruct their lives, I wish that I could reach out and say to each one of them, as one survivor to another: "Look deep within yourself for the strength and courage you may not even know is there. Don't be ashamed or afraid to accept the help and support of family and friends. Depend on the power of faith and hope and love to get you through your dark and trying times."

In the days following the tragedy of September 11, 2001, none of us will ever forget the images of twisted steel, shattered glass, and broken stone. But the foundation of our great country is not built of these materials, but of dreams and ideals that cannot be destroyed. The greatest gift that these survivors can give to their lost child, or lost parent, or lost partner, is the commitment to carry on and keep alive their loved one's wishes, dreams, and ideals . . . for then, they have not died . . . but live on in the hearts and minds of those who love them.

ROBERT NOVAK

Robert Novak is the writer of the political column "Inside Report," one of the longest-running syndicated columns in the nation, and appears on CNN's Evans & Novak. *He is co-executive producer of CNN's* The Capital Gang *and occasional cohost of* Crossfire.

Every day, I ought to give thanks that my four grandparents—my father's parents in Ukraine and my mother's in Lithuania—more than a century ago immigrated to America. They arrived uninvited, penniless, and unable to speak a word of English. The next generation produced college graduates, and I have managed to make a living writing in a language that was foreign to my grandparents.

That's the often-repeated miracle of America. But why did my grandparents travel halfway around the world in steerage to a hard, friendless life in a foreign country? Because they sought freedom. That is why a vast majority of immigrants have come to America in past years, and that is why every national emergency—including the current war against terrorism—is a test for the Republic.

World history records a relentless succession of governments imposing their will over ordinary people. The American Revolution was no mere rebellion by one power faction seeking to replace another, but an assault on the essence of governmental power. Tom Paine and Thomas Jefferson distrusted and feared government, and the Bill of Rights seeks to preserve freedom from the excesses of those who govern. Entering its third century, the American Revolution is unique in maintaining its resistance to governmental power. Coincidentally, that freedom leads to prosperity.

Material gain is why today's immigrants—from German MBAs to Mexican manual workers—clamor to come here. Once here, they can enjoy less interference from the state than in anywhere else in the world.

But "public servants," by their very nature, want to control our lives, and seize on every emergency as a pretext for doing so. So, the September 11 terrorist attacks on America, while understandably intensifying American patriotism, generated new demands for extended governmental power. In seeking heightened security, personal liberties are threatened. More police power and diminished protection of the individual are proposed. The war on terrorism is even cited to promote old statist goals of more government spending, higher taxes, and more intrusive regulation.

What America means to me is freedom, unequaled elsewhere in the world. Protecting it is our essential national priority.

MICHELE O'BRIEN

Michele O'Brien is a registered nurse in New York City.

I am a twenty-nine-year-old registered nurse, and I work in the operating room at a large New York City hospital. I live on the Upper East Side of Manhattan.

I was scheduled to work at three o'clock on September 11, 2001. Upon hearing of the attacks, I immediately reported to work. We were prepared for the worst, for the thousands of victims we would treat, but there was no one to save. This devastating awareness only set in when I worked at Stuyvesant High School on September 13, 2001. The high school had been transformed into a triage center, a fully equipped ER. However, the few patients we treated were rescue workers—police officers, firemen, military personnel, and volunteers. No victims, no survivors. Despite having seen the images of the attacks and of ground zero hundreds of times, it was only when I walked up to the site that I could comprehend the sheer enormity of the disaster, and I knew that the following morning I would have to tell my two sisters that there was no hope for their friends.

For all the sadness and the sorrow I have witnessed in the weeks and months that have passed since September 11, I have also been witness to the extraordinary selflessness, generosity, and kindness that New Yorkers and Americans have extended to each other during this terrible time. People donated clothing, medicine, food, money, time, and even their blood, and they still wanted to know how they could help! Lines to donate blood were longer than any I had ever seen for a concert or sporting event. Whatever their occupation or talent, people used it to help others. The night I spent at Stuyvesant High School, I met many doctors and nurses from all areas of medicine. They had all come from work. Five doctors had driven down from Canada. I met a nurse who had married a New York City firefighter on Saturday; they were on their honeymoon in Florida and drove back. Even on the ride downtown with three NYPD officers that night, we were greeted with homemade banners stating THANK YOU, NYPD and teenagers waving flags and cheering along the West Side Highway.

It's been one year since September 11. I still get a chill when I see a picture of the New York City skyline, but I am warmed by the sense of pride and privilege I feel for being an American, and that "our flag was still there."

GEORGE A. OLAH

George A. Olah was awarded the 1994 Nobel Prize in Chemistry for his contribution to carbocation chemistry.

Four decades ago after the defeat of the 1956 revolution against Soviet dominance, I came as a penniless refugee to North America from my native Hungary. Years later I was asked for a quotation for my listing in *Who's Who in America*. I wrote, "America is still offering a new home and nearly unlimited possibilities to the newcomer who is willing to work hard for it. It is also where the main action in science and technology remains." I still fully believe in what I said. What more can an immigrant ask for, when he and his family found a wonderful new country, for which I am eternally grateful. I have had a most rewarding career in research and teaching, which I still continue. I hope that my work was able to contribute in a small way to the achievements of science and education, essential for the future of our country. It is the uniqueness of America that immigrants can, in a short while, turn into Americans in all senses of the word, and contribute in their own ways to build and strengthen further this great country of ours.

NORMAN ORNSTEIN

Norman Ornstein is a resident scholar at the American Enterprise Institute for Public Policy Research in Washington, D.C., an election analyst for CBS News, and a writer and member of USA Today's *Board of Contributors.*

On the morning of September 11, I drove from my home to Dulles Airport to catch a flight to Norfolk, Virginia, where I was going to address several hundred government ethics officers about the state of ethics in government. The day was beautiful—the sky was crystal blue and as clear as I have ever seen it. I was on the jet way, ready to board the flight, when they called us back. The second plane had hit the World Trade Center, and soon thereafter, the flight from Dulles to Los Angeles, which left not far from my own gate, hit the Pentagon.

I drove home shaking, knowing that we had experienced a devastating terrorist attack, not knowing what would come next, knowing I likely knew somebody who had been killed (two, in fact, on the flight from Dulles), wondering what was to become of our country. Like many others, I called my children, both away at college, as soon as I could get through, just to establish a connection, make sure they were okay, and let them know that we in Washington were okay, too.

I raged at the perpetrators of these unspeakable

acts. I continue to rage. But I knew even then that rage would have to be translated into a careful, cold, and calculated plan for action—that if we lashed out blindly, it would backfire, but that we nonetheless needed to have a targeted and massive response. But we needed a simultaneous, massive move to make sure no additional terrorist acts would take place, and an equally massive move to rebuild the disaster areas and deal with our collective loss.

Rage was joined by pride as the president and the Congress worked over the next weeks to develop the right kind of action plan, not overreacting in reach or scope but asserting the full force of American power in just the right way—and with full bipartisan unity. At the same time, a few senseless, random acts of violence against Muslim Americans (and Sikhs and others mistaken for Muslims) did not cascade into a broad wave of anti-Islamic emotion. American values held firm.

My pride in my country swelled more as I saw all of us—compassionate, caring, and committed—join as brothers and sisters to help recover. I set aside time every day to read the *New York Times* profiles of victims, crying that so many good people had been senselessly lost and their families left bereft.

The Constitution is the bulwark of America's democracy, but a document is only so strong. It must be undergirded by a culture with a set of values that reflect the core principles of the Constitution—and the test comes not in everyday life but under massive stress. We've passed that test, showing yet again that we remain the world's beacon of freedom and decency. Even if some al-Qaeda terrorists and their allies remain alive and plot further inhuman acts, America has beaten them, and not only on the battlefield.

STEVE OSUNSAMI

Steve Osunsami is a news correspondent for ABC's World News Tonight.

Soon after the attacks on New York and Washington, I ran across a number of news articles on the renewed vows, the tighter hugs, and the more heartfelt I-love-you's many Americans were sharing with their loved ones, particularly their wives, husbands, and life partners.

As silly as it sounds, I felt like I had missed out.

As a network news correspondent, I was busy running around the country covering these issues. I didn't have time to be part of the experience. It's a fact about my work that I struggle with: You're required to spend so much of your time "covering" life, sometimes it's difficult to have one of your own.

It's now months since September 11, and I don't quite feel the same. I'm still on the outside of the looking glass, looking in, but what's inside has slowly returned to what I'm used to seeing.

A friend of mine has returned to cheating on his wife. Another lost his job after his employer learned he is gay. And I still can't go to a cocktail party with a white friend, where most of the people there are white, without my friend using my résumé to grease every introduction, simply because I'm black.

Men—and I do take this liberty—mostly men are still terribly unfaithful partners. The complexities of race in this country haven't changed. And you only need to look at the changing priorities of the network and cable newscasts to realize how bored many Americans have become with the patriotism of the fight overseas.

I got the sense that after the attacks, when it came to how we related to one another, we were as close to my ideal as we had ever been. It seemed that by having a common and immediate enemy, more of us were moved to walk hand in hand.

I now realize it was simply a wonderful American moment that was very temporary. And I no longer feel like I missed something grand.

BILL OWENS

Bill Owens is governor of the state of Colorado.

As we mourned the heroes who gave their lives on September 11—and sought to comfort the families who survived them—I found renewed optimism in the strength of the American character and in the principles of family, faith, and freedom.

As with so much in the history of our great country, we learn lessons from the depth of character and the sacrifices of the individuals. Colorado is home to one of the first American soldiers wounded in our war on terrorism. Corporal Christopher Chandler, who was wounded during a minesweeping mission in Afghanistan, reminds us of the extraordinary sacrifices that ordinary Americans have made to preserve our freedom and democracy.

Rather than shred the American fabric of family, faith, and freedom, the terrorist attacks provided us an opportunity to once again celebrate what is good and right and decent about our nation. Through the daily actions of millions of men and women, we have once again demonstrated to the world that the United States is a nation not of buildings and monuments, but of strong and resilient people.

That, to me, is why the American motto *E Pluribus Unum*—"Out of Many, One"—fits the character of our nation so well, and why it still speaks to all of us more than 225 years after it was first chosen.

JACK PAAR

Jack Paar is a television and radio pioneer. He hosted The Tonight Show *from 1957 to 1962.*

How fortunate I am that my great-grandparents came to America and did not get off the wagon in Afghanistan. I would have had to work hard for many years to buy a used donkey, and I am quite sure that you could not teach a camel to chase a ball! I could never wear one of those hats that look like a pancake beret, or live in a country where religious police make sure that women are forced to hide behind their *burqas,* long cloaks that make them look like they are wearing a screen door or a telephone booth with feet.

How damn lucky I am to be an American—especially since I speak English only and drive on the right side of the road. And now to be told, along with millions of others, that I am a part of the Greatest Generation. In my lifetime, I have seen the automobile, airplane, radio, and television, the victory of two world wars, a landing on the moon, atomic energy, and Viagra.

Despite our glorious past, I have a strong, apocalyptic feeling that our future is behind us. The culture has been so changed by greed and tastelessness, a disrespect for law, corrupt politicians and business executives, that we are no longer the respected country that the world envied. We have high school students shooting and killing other students, mothers drowning their children, and a fifteen-year-old boy flying an airplane into a building. There will be others, because more than one jumped over the cuckoo's nest.

We have a strong military, especially in the air, and on the sea, but it appears we have no intelligence on the ground. The CIA, the Secret Service, the FBI never have been very aware of attacks on this country. They missed on Pearl Harbor, although we now know there was much information available. The failure of this country to recognize the recent infiltration of terrorists is sadly ridiculous. The terrorists were undocumented and illegal, taking flying lessons on credit cards, some with driver's licenses.

Our intelligence services did not even know about the invasion from Mars into New Jersey, which Orson Welles reported on his radio program. I was a young radio announcer that night, and I could have alerted the State Department, but I did not want to be pushy. The finest intelligence information is in Israel, the Vatican, and the William Morris office.

I wish to honestly state that we are not as great a nation as our forefathers planned. We have lost the importance of the family; we have lost civility and manners; our literature is not what it was fifty years ago; and music has lost its melody. Lyrics are not to be heard (fortunately), but screamed. I think how many hundreds of years it took to produce a Gershwin, Rodgers and Hammerstein, or Berlin. And yet, many performers fill stadiums by the thousands singing in their underwear or mincing about like a peacock in heat. I do not believe that they could sing such trash standing still, wearing a jacket and tie.

Hollywood produces over a hundred motion pictures a year and, in my view, less than five can be viewed, much less enjoyed, by an intelligent, adult audience. This past year has been the most embarrassing in memory. I wonder if the screenwriters in Hollywood have lost the ability to tell a story! The new cinema is fifty minutes of special effects, violence, and vulgarity, followed by a ten-minute car chase, topped off by the obligatory "body through the glass window." Sometimes, there is ten more minutes for extended kissing and the lighting of cigarettes. (You may have noticed that actors never seem to smoke them, just light them!) More than fifty times a year I turn to my wife and ask, "What the hell was that all about?"

Television has become more and more a commercial medium. It is very common on cable to see the same advertisement three times within a half hour. It's the Yellow Pages with pictures.

In America we can do that sort of thing—and if it's brash, brazen, so what? At least we're free to express ourselves.

GEORGE E. PATAKI

*George E. Pataki is governor of the state
of New York.*

The twenty-first century began with high hopes for a bright future with boundless possibilities for our nation. Now, some may be asking if we still have the faith to feel confident about a century that began in horror, or whether the forces of evil have handed us a somber and uncertain future.

New Yorkers—and indeed all Americans—have already provided us with the answer. Our response since the early morning of September 11 was unequivocal. It was a defining moment that answered the question in no uncertain terms. We will respond to evil with good. We will answer terror with strength. We will meet adversity with resolve. We will defeat hatred with tolerance.

We will rebuild, we will succeed, we will meet tomorrow as we meet today, with the same confidence, the same optimism, and the same belief in the unlimited potential of our future that we had on September 10.

The American spirit was shown to the world on September 11 and the days since. It is an invincible spirit—the incarnation of compassion and courage—tempered, but not harshened . . . tested, but not weakened . . . bent, but not broken.

And because of this spirit, the terrorists failed.

Their goal was not just to destroy two towers and kill thousands, horrible as that was; their goal was to divide us, frighten us, take away our freedom, and weaken our confidence. They failed. New Yorkers and Americans are more unified than ever, more committed to protecting our freedom, and more committed to building a bright future founded upon the very principles the terrorists sought to destroy.

From Valley Forge, to the beaches of Normandy, to the heroes of September 11, Americans have always risen to the occasion to overcome tremendous challenges. Their examples of sacrifice and determination should not only fill us with a great sense of pride in our heritage but also with a tremendous sense of confidence and optimism as we look to meet the challenges of the future.

ROSS PEROT

Ross Perot is a Texas businessman, who, after turning his Electronic Data Systems into a multi-billion-dollar corporation, became one of the richest men in America. He ran unsuccessfully as a Reform Party candidate in the 1992 presidential election.

As a small boy in the 1930s in Texas during the Depression, I was going through a trunk in the attic of our home. This trunk contained a military uniform, helmet, and other equipment that had belonged to my uncle, Keller Hoffman, who was killed by mustard gas in World War I. His wife, Oma (my father's sister), and her two little boys, Keller and Perot, were left alone to fend for themselves and had to grow up without a father. This made a lasting impression on me. The sacrifices made by others give us the freedom that many of us take for granted.

Bill Leftwich was one of my close friends at the Naval Academy. He came from a prominent family in Memphis, Tennessee. Bill joined the Marine Corps on graduation and fought heroically in Vietnam. He received the Navy Cross during his first tour. Bill was so outstanding he was made aide to John Warner, assistant secretary of the navy.

At the end of his tour, John Warner said, "Bill, you

can go anywhere you want. Where do you want to go?"

Bill replied, "Back to Vietnam."

Bill was in charge of a reconnaissance battalion, and it was his policy, not Marine Corps policy, to personally rescue any recon team that got into trouble. One team did get into trouble. Bill successfully extracted the team from the jungle. The helicopter elevated 1,200 feet above the ground, and the helicopter blade hit the edge of the cliff.

As the helicopter fluttered to the ground to crash, Bill, with no emotion in his voice, used his command center radio to dictate a farewell message to his wife and two sons.

There is a large, bronze Leftwich memorial located at Quantico, Virginia. A miniature of this statue, the Leftwich trophy, is given each year to the most outstanding young marine officer. Bill Leftwich gave his life so that you and I can be free.

My roommate at the Naval Academy was Lyle Armel. He was so outstanding, he was chosen as aide to Admiral Burke. Lyle served on the River Patrol in Vietnam, where huge amounts of Agent Orange had been spread. He was able to complete his navy career even though he had significant health problems.

I visited him as he was dying of cancer from Agent Orange. He could not have been more positive. His exact words were "Think about all of our friends who were killed in combat. I got to come home and see my children grow up!" Lyle gave his life to preserve our freedom.

Alex Hottell, a West Point graduate and Rhodes scholar, was a helicopter pilot in Vietnam. He was killed in action in 1970. Before his death, he wrote his own obituary, stating, "I am the best authority on my own life." The entire obituary was printed in the *New York Times*. His single most important message was "I didn't die for my country. I lived for my country. If there is nothing worth living for, there is nothing worth dying for."

Nick Rowe was a West Point graduate. His children's pictures are in my office. He was the only POW ever to escape from Vietnam. A Vietnamese guard was escorting him to another location when an American helicopter flew over. Nick knocked the guard unconscious and ran out into an open field, waving to the helicopter. The pilot initially thought he was Vietnamese but decided to swoop down to see what was happening. He recognized that Nick was an American, landed, and rescued him. Nick came back to the United States, remained on active duty, and was sent to the Philippines on a classified assignment. Nick was assassinated in the Philippines. His children grew up without a father. Certainly Nick Rowe paid a huge price for our freedom.

* * *

During the Vietnam War, President Nixon asked me to lead a project to embarrass the Vietnamese into changing their brutal treatment of our POWs. On one occasion as we were flying out of a refugee camp in a remote area of Laos, I heard a pinging sound and asked the flight crew, "What's that?"

They replied, "Ground fire hitting the wings." Fortunately, the plane was able to continue to fly.

On another occasion I was flying in an Air America Cessna aircraft in the middle of the night, over triple-canopy jungles, from Vientiane, Laos, to Bangkok, Thailand. I was asleep, leaning against the door. Suddenly the door blew off and I woke up hanging by my seat belt. I pulled myself back inside the cockpit and we later landed safely in Bangkok. Events like these help one appreciate just how precious freedom is and that it does exact a price.

Two of my employees, who were working on a large computer project in Iran, were taken hostage during the Iranian Revolution in 1979. The reason the Iranians took them hostage was to ensure that our team remained in Iran during the revolution, to keep the computers in operation.

Our government was unable to help in any way.

I asked Colonel Bull Simons to organize a rescue team to extract our men. Colonel Bull Simons was a legendary member of the Special Forces. He led the Son Tay raid twenty miles outside of Hanoi in 1970.

He organized the team and put it in place in Tehran.

He sent me back from Tehran to have a rescue team on the border of Turkey, in case our team in Tehran needed help.

Unfortunately, I visited the U.S. embassy before leaving Tehran, and within hours the Iranians were tearing up the city looking for me. We learned they had my picture at the airport.

I waited until ten minutes before the plane was scheduled to take off before checking in. As I went to the ticket counter, the agent was reading a book, and even though my picture was on her desk, she never looked at it. The plane was delayed for five hours, and I sat within thirty feet of the ticket agent who had my picture in front of her. During those five hours, I was reminded how special and fragile freedom is.

Colonel Simons staged the largest jailbreak in the history of Tehran, with a team of Vietnam veterans who worked in my company. He brought them all safely to the Turkish border, 540 miles across Tehran. Freedom has a very special meaning to the two men who had been in prison and our entire rescue team. Freedom has a taste to those who fought and almost died, that the protected will never know.

REGIS PHILBIN

Regis Philbin is cohost of ABC's Live with Regis and Kelly *and host of* Who Wants to Be a Millionaire.

I watched those planes go into the World Trade Center. I experienced the feelings of sorrow, doubt, and fear immediately afterward. I wondered what's next and when is it coming? Now, months later, I feel terribly proud of our country and the people who live here. We have survived the most savage attack on our nation in modern times and have answered it swiftly and bravely. From the president to the firefighter in his fire station waiting for the bell to ring, I am so impressed with us. It's a challenging and exciting time to be an American. I used to wonder if we had the guts and character of our predecessors. I don't anymore.

GEORGE PICKETT

George Pickett was a member of the New York City Fire Department, 1968–1990, and is presently a firefighter in Arizona. He is one of the most experienced fire officers in the United States.

THE BRAVE

It came with shock and grief that we saw images of innocent civilians slaughtered on September 11, 2001. With them, 343 of my fellow firefighters died heroic deaths at the World Trade Center. Wars can last months or years, stunning atrocities can last moments. Will we remember those members of FDNY who died there? I am haunted by that terrible act, but I can't forget that death, danger, and destruction in our own streets and countryside are ever present, day and night. These domestic street wars and the domestic violence kill, maim, and prey on all citizens, and are daily faced by the Brave—the firefighters of America. My own years in the Lower East Side of Manhattan as a rookie followed by hard-earned promotions through the ranks taught me dedication, courage, and loyalty to America and to the FDNY. Loyalty is overwhelmed by duty when the bells ring, and sometimes the members do not return home.

Firefighters are this nation's first responders and often find horrific conditions when they arrive on the scene. Through desperate encounters with danger they ply their trade for the love of the job and often take home memories of death and injuries of their fellow man that are permanently engraved on their souls.

My brothers and sisters of the Fire Service, with heads held high, expect the worst. Firefighters have feelings, never doubt that, a great deal of feelings. I remember perilously bailing out of a fire-ravaged tenement in Hell's Hundred Acres, leaping at the last moment to escape death into the bucket of a tower ladder, itself shrouded in flames. I heard the screams of young children inside the burning room as I swung the apparatus away from the flames and sobbed. My sobs were for the pitiful children, of course, but in equal measure for my own miserable, unforgivable failure. The plaintive, imploring death cries of those little ones would remain in my memory as vividly as the cries of life from my newborn after their natural childbirth. I can't name any firefighter in the world who doesn't share that very attitude, not one.

I stand a little taller now, as all Americans and firefighters do, and display my flag more proudly, as I remember those courageous people who died on September 11. Now those citizens and other emergency workers will be heroes forever. We are united now; we have discovered we are one. We know the greatness of our America lies not in our many bounties, but in our people and in the deeds we do. We must never forget the bravery, among and within us. My America, you will always be the land of the free, and the home of the brave.

STANLEY B. PRUSINER

Dr. Stanley B. Prusiner was awarded the 1997 Nobel Prize in Medicine for his discovery of prions. He is the director of the Institute for Neurodegenerative Disease at the University of California, San Francisco.

ONLY IN AMERICA—LAND OF OPPORTUNITY

Only in America could I have had the opportunity to discover prions. What are prions and why only in America? Prions are infectious agents that multiply yet they are composed only of protein; in other words, prions are infectious proteins. Prions have neither DNA nor RNA, the genetic material of life, so they differ profoundly from all other infectious pathogens, including viruses, bacteria, parasites, and fungi. The most well-known prions are those causing mad cow disease; they also cause scrapie in sheep and Creutzfeldt-Jakob disease (CJD) in people. All three of these disorders are degenerative diseases of the brain.

Only in America were the resources available that I needed to perform the scientific research that led to the discovery of prions. Nowhere on our planet is scientific discovery so well supported as in America. And only in America is the award of grant funds from agencies like the National Institutes of Health (NIH) and the National Science Foundation (NSF) decided by panels of scientific peers whose decisions are based on the merit of the proposed science. While the granting process is not perfect, it functions much better than most government-sponsored programs both here and abroad.

My scientific training began at the University of Pennsylvania and continued later at the University of Stockholm, the University of California, San Francisco (UCSF), and the NIH. The opportunity to do research both as an undergraduate and a medical student at the University of Pennsylvania helped forge a career that was unplanned. The egalitarian nature of our society allowed me to gain an education at an outstanding university, having come from a public high school where I had a less than stellar record. As my commitment to biomedical research blossomed, a remarkable opportunity was presented to me. I was able to fulfill my military commitment at the height of the Vietnam War by enlisting in the Public Health Service and doing research at the NIH. While I worked at the NIH, I learned how to purify proteins from bacteria and how to scale up the preparations. These skills were to prove invaluable later as I explored the cause of scrapie. Only in America would I have been able to fashion a residency training program in neurology that allowed me to focus on finding a worthwhile research question. While caring for a patient with CJD, I became fascinated by the mysteries surrounding the cause of CJD and scrapie. After two years of clinical training in neurology at UCSF, I set up a laboratory there and devoted all my effort to identifying the particle that causes scrapie.

Government grants as well as private philanthropy made possible my work first on scrapie and later on mad cow disease and CJD. Only in America could a young assistant professor with seemingly crazy ideas gain sufficient funding from the NIH and the NSF to begin studying a slow-developing disease like scrapie. Only in America could I obtain the additional monies required for this work from private donors and foundations. The philanthropic support of science in America has been encouraged by some enlightened sections of our tax code. Without such support from private sources, I would have never been able to assemble the personnel, equipment, and facilities needed for the discovery of prions. Without the extraordinary scientific talent that populates the San Francisco Bay Area, I would not have been able to hire the skilled personnel required to perform the necessary research.

Only in America was the opportunity there for me to climb from a rather humble beginning in Des Moines, Iowa, and later Cincinnati, Ohio, to the dizzying heights of scientific accomplishment. Three of my four grandparents were born in Europe. They all immigrated to America with few resources except their will to forge a better life. America gave them the opportunity, it gave my parents the opportunity, it gave me the opportunity, and it is now giving my children similar opportunities.

SALLY QUINN

Sally Quinn is a reporter for The Washington Post.

I am an army brat. My father was in the infantry and fought in both World War II and the Korean War. I grew up on army posts all over the world so I was surrounded from the time I was a child with all the symbols of patriotism. There were American flags everywhere. We always said the Pledge of Allegiance in school and sang the national anthem constantly. I think I must have learned the words to that song before I learned "Happy Birthday." In the mornings there was reveille and the raising of the flag, and in the evening taps and the lowering of the flag. We put our hands over our hearts when we saw the Stars and Stripes. As children we were taught that our fathers were serving in the military and were prepared to die for their country if need be.

Naturally I absorbed all of this and I think it is no accident that I chose to live in Washington, D.C. I confess to tearing up when I hear "The Star-Spangled Banner" and when I see the flag. And I never cease to be inspired by the monuments in this city, from the Lincoln Memorial to the Washington Monument to the Capitol to Arlington Cemetery, where my father is buried.

But those are not just symbols or monuments to me. They are all stories, stories about real people who did noble and brave things to create the most just, democratic, decent society that the world has ever known. I can't look at the flag or hear the anthem or see the monuments without being amazed at the courage and fortitude and especially the vision our forebears had even to conceive of a country and a society like ours. There is never a day that I don't think how lucky and proud I am to be an American. The monuments and symbols also stand to remind us, too, about the importance of the values and morals upon which our country is based. Equality is an easy concept to envision, but when you look at how hard it has been to achieve, certainly in our own but especially in other countries, it is extraordinary.

I have lived through the air-raid drills in Washington during the 1950s and lived in the war-torn countries of Japan and Germany after World War II and during the Korean War, so I have been close to war if not in it. But I had never felt as personally threatened before as I did after September 11. It was interesting to me to observe my own reactions and those of others in the same situation. Even though I was scared—we all were—there was never a moment's doubt in my mind that we would prevail, that our country would get control of the situation, that we would never be vanquished. Watching the brave people who went to the rescue of others that day and in the days afterward made me even more certain. There is a resolve in the American people today that I haven't seen since I was a small child during World War II, and a sense of patriotism that I haven't ever seen except on military posts. It seems that now the whole country is seeing America the way I was brought up to see it and to feel about it.

People talk about the last few decades, which have seemed at times to be devoted to narcissism and self-gratification, and they have despaired. But I never did. I always believed that we go through cycles, and that we have just come out of one and into a cycle of caring for each other and our country in a way that most of us in our lifetimes have never experienced.

Now I don't have to live on an army post to look out my window and see a flag; they are everywhere. And I don't have to go to a football game to hear the national anthem either. You can't turn on the radio or TV without hearing them "playing our song." So nothing has changed for me except to see the whole country rally to one cause—"liberty and justice for all." And it is thrilling.

SALLY JESSE RAPHAEL

Sally Jesse Raphael is host of The Sally Show, *the longest-running talk show on the air.*

We are family! That thought has followed me everywhere I've gone in the days following September 11. We may fight among ourselves, but in the way that family members argue. A particular trait or point of view of one may be particularly annoying, even aberrant, to another. But we are family. And, as with most vibrant, loving, argumentative, passionate families, it becomes instantly clear, after an attack from outside, that we are of one purpose. We all stick together. We stick up for one another. We can rush in to help, with no thought for our own safety . . . because we are family.

This is true on levels that are both noble and humble: noble, as in the ultimate sacrifices made by our police, firefighters, military, and the passengers on the flight in Pennsylvania, who joined valiantly like brothers against their common foe; humble, in the ways that people are now kind to one another, in the grocery store, at the post office, in the elevator, on the highway. Each of us is sensitive to the possibility that the person in front of us may have suffered a loss, as my family did. We speak more freely with strangers, unafraid, and are gentle with one another, because of one stunningly simple realization: We are family.

We look at our women and see those mothers, wives, sisters, daughters, and friends who died in the World Trade Center, or the Pentagon, or on the planes, and each of us experiences firsthand the bottomless holes that have been left in the lives of so many who've lost loved ones. My own daughter, who'd given birth just a few weeks before, lost her best friend in the World Trade Center, a beautiful, intelligent young woman from another country. My daughter held a funeral for her, and sixty-five strangers gathered to mourn as one family. These days, we put our arms a little tighter around the women in our lives, realizing how, in an instant, everything can change. We look at our men and see those fathers, husbands, brothers, sons, and friends who died, all on the same tragic day in September, and we hold on as if we will never let go.

And then, we rally. We look at the strengths of our great nation, and call upon each of our family members to use their particular skill or talent to close the gap, heal the wound, find the enemy, and keep the family functioning at the same time. This family has so many strengths: our ability to fight with valor, cunning, and skill; our inventiveness in creating the highest technology known to man; our statesmanship, in recognizing the need not just to fight terrorism, but to eradicate its causes; our uniquely American birthright, which makes us heir to the idea of unlimited possibilities.

What is perhaps most enlightening about all that

America has been through in the past few months is the collective realization that we are not immune. We now know what it is to experience what other human beings have been facing in their homelands since time began, the realization that we are all vulnerable. The question is never "Why me?" The question is "Why not?" And once again, Americans begin to reinvent themselves, slowly coming to understand that, if our brothers and sisters on the other side of the world are suffering, it is a matter that concerns us directly and calls upon us each to do what we can to ease that suffering. Because when it comes to human beings all over this planet, there is no avoiding the obvious: We are family!

ANN W. RICHARDS

Ann W. Richards is a former governor of the state of Texas.

I was in Dallas on November 22 when John Kennedy was killed. I was in New York on September 11 when the World Trade Center was attacked. On both occasions, my first thought was, I must get home.

In reality or in reverie, we all have a familiar safe-hold called "home," a place that affords the comfort of security, the love of family and friends, and reassurance that everything will be all right. I have read articles about astronauts who turn and look back at our "big blue marble" and have a sensation of longing for home.

The September attacks were individually disturbing to all of us because they violated our home. History had taught us that our country was safe—that the only real threat to our safety could come from within. Now, suddenly, our home was vulnerable to the destructive madness of strangers.

Heartbroken and angry, we wanted to demonstrate that we were determined to protect our home. Flags sprouted on lapels and car antennas. "God Bless America" was on the radio for the first time in years. Millions of dollars poured into relief funds. We were trying to tell everyone that America is our home, and an assault against it is an assault against every one of us.

Like most people, I am frustrated by simplistic, symbolic flag-waving. And yet, we have so few ways to say how much we love America.

To me, this country is about much more than symbolism. It is living testimony to the capacity of human beings to govern themselves and use government for the betterment of the human condition.

I am grateful that I had the good fortune to be born in this country and that, as citizens of the United States, my children, grandchildren, and I enjoy a level of freedom that is unmatched: the freedom to speak as we please, to assemble as we please, to worship as we please, to write as we please, to come and go as we please, to live as we please. I am embarrassed to admit that it takes a tragedy to make me consciously aware of how precious my home, America, is to me.

ORAL ROBERTS

Oral Roberts is an evangelist, and founder and chancellor of Oral Roberts University in Tulsa, Oklahoma.

September 11, 2001, abruptly and deeply reawakened in me the supreme honor and glory of being born an American.

As an author, educator, and evangelist, I've traveled this nation, met the people, given my ministry, met the successes and defeats head-on, but ended up feeling the very soul of our people.

I saw the depths of the inner man of hundreds of thousands face-to-face, and millions more who wrote to me about their dreams and heartaches and requests for any spiritual help I could give them.

September 11 shook me and made me realize that what I had seen and felt was really true. The character, the deep faith, the unwavering values in a changing society emerged real and tangible.

My feeling is we've suffered a terrible temporary loss but an almost supernatural awakening as to who we really are, and what we have lived and fought and died for is as real as life itself. And through our president, George W. Bush, we have taken our stand:

We will not be intimidated.
We will not be destroyed.

We will save our souls and
  our freedoms and security.

While I hurt for those who were hurt and those who were killed, and pray for them constantly, I feel a surge of new hope greater than I've known in my entire life as an American.

The seventy nations I've preached in during these fifty-four years of my ministry are very important because of the people. But to me the people of our country have a faith in God, roots in decency and value of life, and a vision for greatness and goodness exceeding them all.

My prayer is that I, and every American, will seize the moment and, more than that, *grow* in all that we hold dear in the precious and glorious country we call America and our home.

CLIFF ROBERTSON

Cliff Robertson is an actor.

I was indeed in a unique observation post at seven thousand feet above the tip of Manhattan. I indeed did see both initial explosions fifteen minutes apart. I did not realize or even surmise the severity of the situation. And therein, I suspect, an analogy might be drawn. In our hermetically sealed American environment, we have a tendency to think "that has *not* happened—*will* not happen." That is because for over two hundred years, there has been a barrier from Europe and Asia—an invisible, invincible shield, if you will. That we are the perpetual "good guy." That God is on *our* side, and that he will not let continuous harm touch our pristine shores. That we, in our eternally optimistic youth as a nation, feel protected by our "goodness" and God. Ergo the analogy.

Because I had never heard Air Traffic Control bark that unfamiliar phrase, "Land at the nearest airport—this is a national emergency," a surreal dimension descended upon me at 9:05 A.M. that crystalline morning headed alone for the West Coast. That surreal curtain has only just begun to lift. I am but one in an audience of over 200 million whose disbelief has been suspended. America—this sleeping giant—has been given a wake-up call and is only beginning to smell the coffee. Lest the infidels who have shaken us from our naive slumber believe that the sleeping giant will simply and briefly yawn and return to its slumber—a warning.

We were awakened other times—witness December 7, 1941. And we did not turn our backs; nor will we turn our back to this reality. History may well report that the infidels came just in time—just in time to keep this great nation awake, alert, and aware of its dangers and its responsibilities, responsibilities not only to this bastion of freedom, but responsibilities to freedom-seeking peoples everywhere.

NED ROREM

Ned Rorem is an author and composer.

When a moth drowns in Africa, a sycamore in Oregon trembles, however faintly. No man is an island, all life is interconnected; events of September 11 confirmed this definitively. Many an artist on that day considered: What difference now do my so-called creative acts make? But a week later he knew: They make all the difference. For our civilization will be judged in the future, as it has always been judged in the past, by its arts and not by its armies—by construction more than by destruction. The art, no matter its theme or language, by definition reflects the time: A waltz in a moment of tragedy, or a dirge during prosperity, may come into focus only a century later. As a Quaker I was raised to believe that there is no alternative to peace. Perhaps it's wrong, perhaps right, but I am not ashamed of this belief. Art, no matter how violent-seeming, is an extension of peace.

JOHN G. ROWLAND

John G. Rowland is governor of the state of Connecticut.

During the Revolution, our leaders were farmers who left their plows and picked up their rifles and ran to fight for freedom.

Today, the true leaders are the firemen and police officers who rushed to aid their neighbors in New York City. The true leaders are the National Guard troops who have stepped up for duty in this country and overseas. The true leaders are the postal workers who found themselves on the front lines of this new war.

The true leaders are the volunteers who have set aside their own grief to console those whose lives were forever changed on that sunny Tuesday morning.

Evil struck our country. Our response has been equal parts strength, bravery, compassion, and love.

And that response shows *why* we *will* prevail.

The moment those horrific acts occurred was a defining moment, a moment contained within the long history of a freedom-loving nation. A nation that won two world wars, took down the Berlin Wall, and parted the Iron Curtain.

Now we are showing that we are still a strong nation, united in spirit and resolve.

We have drawn strength from our heritage. Each

flag we pass on the highway, each homemade sign, reminds us of our heroes, and what they fight and have fought for. Our history sustains us.

And we have become a more compassionate people, a more caring people. We have become, more than in recent times, a community.

We found, in the outpouring of support we saw in the days after the attacks, the *true* face of the American people.

MARK RUSSELL

Mark Russell is a political satirist.

I live in Washington, D.C., and the instant the city was in terrifying danger on September 11, it lost its image of a bureaucratic enclave devoid of "real Americans," at least temporarily. In the following weeks, cultural differences were set aside as all Americans assumed a common classification. Each of us—firefighter, bassoon player, busboy, soccer coach, waiter, and systems analyst—was a target. Every American was now a "real American" and every American was a bull's-eye.

We are not literally the *United States* all that often. On those rare occasions when we share a common emotion, during the Academy Awards, the Super Bowl, or a juicy criminal trial, rednecks and socialites alike gawk at the event as an innocent diversion. September 11 and its ghastly fallout was and is another shared moment of a sadly different kind.

We and our fellow targets surprised each other in those first days in strange ways. Yielding to others in rush-hour traffic was one. I could not believe my own completely uncharacteristically calm and uncomplaining demeanor in airports. I also experienced a behavior pattern for which in another circumstance I might have sought professional counseling: I was agreeing with everything a president of the United States was doing and saying! We saw bipartisan unity of all things in Congress as the members stood on the steps of the Capitol and sang "God Bless America." That unity was good while it lasted. It broke down right around "white with foam." Congress soon resumed its usual bickering and so have the rest of us, for that matter, which means we are back to normal. Sort of.

As I write this months later, I know that this country's rock-hard strength lies in our capability of surprising ourselves as we did during those tough days. When people are crushed by draconian rituals of fundamentalist rigidity, there are no such surprises.

I hope we have seen the end of that corny old campaign rhetoric about the only real Americans being in the heartland. Well, New York City is the heartland. Washington, D.C., is the heartland. The heartland is in each of the fifty stars on our flag.

Incidentally, I am back to not always agreeing with the president. Still, last September my short-lived approval felt kind of nice.

GEORGE H. RYAN

George H. Ryan is governor of the state of Illinois.

I believe there is a confidence, a swagger, an understanding that is distinctly American that you do not see and cannot find anywhere else. As a people, we succeed because our forefathers established not just a country or a government, but a new way of thinking. Throughout our history, we have groused at each other and complained to and about each other. We pick fights and we seem to be anything but united. America will always be this way. But we are united as a people because we all understand that our differences are the foundation of our strength as a nation. Americans know inherently that we do not easily give in or give up. To protect our strength, we must protect our differences. I don't know of many other nations on earth that have been able to strike that balance. I'm glad that I live in one of them.

DIANE SAWYER

Diane Sawyer is the award-winning coanchor of ABC News' Good Morning America *and* PrimeTime Thursday.

My America is filled with the music of Kentucky and its rolling hills, the Thoroughbreds grazing over the horizons, the low orange sun dipping behind the bluegrass. Country ham, okra, and our family toasts and stories. My mother's refrigerator—the collard greens, Benedictine dip, meat loaf, and chess pie.

Reporters always talk about the central, unifying experience of Middle America in the 1950s and early 1960s. A lot of us were the grandchildren of farmers making our way into the big city with a sense of wonder, and possibility. Behind us, the security of community—back when so many of us grilled Velveeta and watched the same television shows. Ahead of us, the discovery that America also had to change to stay great—from race, to the power of women, to a rededicated sense of family.

I was at ground zero on September 11 when everything changed and yet the main thing did not: the profound heart of the country. I once heard Ronald Reagan say that as far as he knew America is the only country whose national anthem ends with a question mark. That's who Americans still are to me: seekers, questioners, explorers, heading out to the horizon and then returning to the place we know, and seeing it again, always, for the first time.

LAURA SCHLESSINGER

Dr. Laura Schlessinger, licensed marriage, family, and child counselor, is a radio talk-show host and best-selling author. She is known as "Dr. Laura," and her nationally syndicated talk-radio program is the fastest growing in radio history, with over 15 million listeners.

When I received the request for this essay, I was overwhelmed. How does one condense such passion and philosophy into a few paragraphs? Then, when I sat down to compose my thoughts, the answer came simply, if not ironically, following September 11. Safety—America means *safety* to me.

Each time I leave America to travel to other countries, I am afraid. At the end of the trip, coming through U.S. Customs and in plain sight of hundreds of people, I drop to my knees and kiss the American ground. Here in America—home—I feel safe.

And September 11 didn't change that feeling in any fundamental way. Of course I, like everyone else, fear terrorist attacks.

But that is not the worst fear to have. It is worse to live under tyranny. It is worse to be intentionally starved of food and opportunity by a government that is incompetent, corrupt, or evil. It is worse, ultimately, to live without hope.

In truth, though, I was fearful here in America

until September 11. Right here in America many people have been afraid to speak their minds in public about God, religion, traditional family values, and patriotism. They feared the fierce and debilitating backlash from the apparent victors in the so-called culture wars. Amazingly, September 11 galvanized many Americans to reaffirm the guaranteed safety of free speech in America, to reclaim the values and principles that gave birth to American ideals, to act with the courage of their convictions.

America is not just a place. It is a place founded on a purpose—the purpose is the promise of safety to every individual. But as individuals we must join together to protect America *as a whole*. We must rededicate ourselves as a nation to keep American ideals alive and secure.

There isn't one single time I hear "The Star-Spangled Banner" that I don't well up with emotion and tears. I am so proud—and so grateful—to be an American.

Harrison H. Schmitt

Former NASA astronaut Harrison H. Schmitt was lunar module pilot on Apollo 17, *the final Apollo moon mission, and the only geologist to explore the lunar surface. He also served as United States senator from New Mexico.*

Immigrants have forged and tempered America. They and their descendants continue to hammer, shape, and sharpen the working tools of democracy. For at least twelve thousand years and possibly longer, North America has been a haven for human beings seeking better and freer lives. These hopeful wanderers combined to create and sustain the United States of America and to defend freedom for 225 years. Late in the twentieth century, the progeny of the immigrants to America helped begin the extension of freedom into outer space. The Apollo landings on the moon, completed with the flight of *Apollo 17* in December 1972, have provided this new opportunity. As the founders recognized in their time of western exploration, today's Americans must ensure that the benefits from deep space exploration reach fruition early in this, the twenty-first century.

With the success of the American Revolution and the wisdom of the founders, the United States became a culturally diverse homeland for immigrants seeking greater freedom. As a result, Americans constitute a unique aggregation of special people and ideas. The cultural and genetic pool that constitutes "Americans" represents the legacy of those with the desire and initiative to leave their homes throughout the world, to survive, and to seek greater personal, political, and economic freedom in this new land.

The creation and preservation of the United States of America form part of humankind's hard-fought ascension toward a society founded on individual freedom. This societal ideal is not the individual freedom of anarchy but one that requires a stable association of the freedoms of all citizens. What better proofs of our progress exist than the continued desire of millions to immigrate to our shores and across our borders, and the continued enmity of those threatened by our example?

With all its imperfections, the overall success of American society is obvious relative to the rest of humanity. Indeed, that success has again and again enabled the defeat of the evil of authoritarianism in the former homelands of ancestral immigrants. The gifts of the founders show that they fully understood our continuing experiment in freedom. Modern history further demonstrates that infinite room exists for improvement in how we use the constitutional and moral tools they provided.

Americans, ironically, will become the new immigrants, going first to the moon, then to Mars, and then beyond, crossing space as their ancestors crossed the Great Plains, mountains, and deserts of their homeland. The incentives to immigrate already exist in the minds of many young Americans and in the energy resources of the moon. Lunar resources not only will help preserve Earth's environment but will support the settlement of the solar system and a replication of freedom beyond Earth. *Apollo 17* was not the last human visit to deep space by free peoples, merely the most recent.

PATRICIA S. SCHROEDER

Patricia S. Schroeder is president and CEO of the Association of American Publishers, Inc. She is a former member of Congress.

This sixty-one-year-old woman, who spent twenty-four years in public service, views the aftermath of the tragic September 11, 2001, events with both celebration and concern. I always thought that to say that America was just a souped-up consumer culture where citizens only cared for themselves was wrong. Indeed, actions following the horror fractured that stereotype. Civic involvement soared and those wonderful public servants that had been the topic of jokes became national heroes. Americans had not lost their souls to consumerism. We deeply care for each other. I celebrate that.

Here is my concern. I love this country deeply. Had I been born in many other countries and lived the life I have lived, I would be in jail or dead. One of my favorite quotes is from our fifteenth president, James Buchanan, who said, "I like the noise of democracy." I'm with President Buchanan and love the noise of democracy. I don't think we would have thrived and developed as we have without that noise. I fear the noise has subsided. People are so worried about public sensitivity; I call it "Patriotic Correctness."

White House spokesman Ari Fleischer said, "People should watch what they say." Wow! Have any of us a corner on truth? Would this nation have been able to grow and refresh its institutions to meet changing needs without vigorous debate and discourse? Americans understand the importance of a broad tolerance of divergent points of view. We welcome new citizens and new ideas and keep retooling our society to incorporate them. There is no question that such robust public discourse is messy, but also no question that it is essential to remaining a vibrant, viable society. My concern is the quieting of democratic noise after the tragedies. Bring it back!

CHARLES E. SCHUMER

*Charles E. Schumer is a United States senator
representing New York State.*

Within hours of the September 11 tragedy, I was
told of a merchant whose store was on the path
heading north from the World Trade Center. He
owned a shoe store, and he stood outside and gave
sneakers to the many women who were fleeing. Just
handing out sneakers—tennis shoes—because he
knew they couldn't run in their high heels.

A civilian hero. That's what I'd call this man. I'm
proud of him, but I'm more proud to say that he's
one of a full army of civilians who charged themselves with serving above and beyond the call of
duty in the wake of September 11.

Thousands of people donated their time, money,
muscle, and sweat to aid in the 9/11 rescue efforts.
Thousands more lined Manhattan's West Side
Highway to cheer the rescue workers as they sped
by, while so many others lined up in front of hospitals, waiting for hours on end to donate blood. Fire-
houses were filled with bouquets of flowers, and,
from what I could tell, platter after platter of
lasagna. And it seems like nearly every storefront,
car window, front yard, and balcony has proudly
displayed the American flag at one time or another.

I've heard tale after tale of not just my fellow New
Yorkers but Americans from one end of the country

to the other who have extended a hand and thus pulled our nation closer together. We have unified across so many lines that often divide us. Volunteering together, working together, grieving together—we are truly one.

When America awoke on the morning of September 12, we woke up in a new America, a new world, and a new era of conflict. The events of 9/11 will never leave us the same—not as individuals, not as New Yorkers, not as Americans, not as world citizens. But we have learned from it all as we grieved, and I believe that during this time of crisis, we've actually changed the way we treat each other.

The best way to honor and remember those lost on September 11 is by keeping it that way.

DIANA L. SCHWARZBEIN

Diana L. Schwarzbein, M.D., is founder of the Endocrinology Institute of Santa Barbara and a recognized expert on preventive medicine, metabolic healing, and hormone replacement therapy.

Freedom is the one word that represents what is most important to me as well as what my country means to me in these times of heightened awareness. I believe that this country is so great because of my rights to intellectual and personal freedom, rights that I so dearly want to keep.

The freedom of speech, the freedom to listen to or play music, the freedom of thought, the freedom to travel, the freedom to dress and look any way I want to without being beaten to death. The freedom to think outside the box. The freedom to choose whom I will be married to, or if I will marry at all. The freedom to be me as long as I am not trying to harm anyone else. The freedom of not being afraid that I may be blown up at any minute.

I am not overly concerned about the possibility of the government listening in on my phone conversations or even having access to my financial statements; after all, I pay taxes every year and report it anyway. So, even though I do not particularly like the idea of someone checking up on me, since I have nothing to hide this type of privacy is not what is the most important thing to me. I want our country to get the "bad" guys so that my freedom of life, and yours too, is not taken away. This is the most important thing to me. If losing some of my right to privacy is the price I need to pay for living freely, I will gladly pay it. And you know what is so great about this country? Because you are an American you have the freedom to disagree with what I just said.

WILLARD SCOTT

Willard Scott is a weather reporter for NBC News' Today.

SOME THOUGHTS ON AMERICA AND AMERICANS

During my stint as weather reporter for the *Today* show on NBC-TV during the past twenty years, I've traveled all across America numerous times. I've done live reports from every state in the union, often from different locations in that same state, giving me a rare and privileged look at our nation and our people. I'd like to share a few of my thoughts and observations with you. Keep in mind these are my thoughts and opinions. (This is my disclaimer in case you don't agree.)

Thought #1: There is no question: we are unequaled in our military powers and our technology. However, I've felt all along that our greatest asset has always been our American agriculture. No people have been blessed with such a wide variety of geography and climates, not to mention the work ethic and the skills of our American farmers. As I was raised for a good deal of my life on a dairy farm, I may be just a tad impartial here. I am very sad at the thought that each year there are fewer and fewer family farms. Nonetheless, the productivity of the agribusiness has allowed us not only to produce enough food to feed us, but indeed, to have the capability to feed the entire world on a relatively small percentage of our land.

Thought #2: Each year we seem to be more and more interested in our past, a truly important ingredient in our natural strength. David McCullough's book on John Adams, Civil War reenactments with more and more people participating in more and more events, movies such as *Pearl Harbor* and *Saving Private Ryan,* and Ken Burns's excellent and graphic productions are all witness to this new and renewed interest in our history. Even the national tragedy of slavery is causing us to look again at our past. And while we see some of our most influential and important Founding Fathers as slaveholders, we are reexamining their character and their contribution, causing us to focus again on our past. The past is without question the prologue to the future, so the people of a great nation must know who they are and where they came from.

Thought #3: My family were all immigrants. They came to America around 1750 and all settled in western North Carolina. Now unless your parents are Native Americans, you came from immigrant stock also. It is my strong belief that the very heart and soul of our American greatness lies in our diversity, our diversity of people and culture. All new groups as they have come to our shores have had to pay their dues. The Irish and the Italians, the Asians, the blacks, and more recently the Hispanics have all had to earn their place in America. No one is owed anything. They have had to endure hardship, prejudice, and hard work to get where they are. What we have in our very diversified population is a culture, made up of many other cultures from all over the world, that becomes uniquely American. The love of country and the pride of citizenship derived from these people give the United States a dedication, loyalty, and patriotic fervor no other nation in the world has.

Travel this land, these United States, as I have the pleasure of doing, and see for yourself.

WINSTON E. SCOTT

Captain Winston E. Scott (USN-Ret.) is a former NASA astronaut. He retired from NASA and the U.S. Navy in 1999 to serve as vice president for student affairs at his alma mater, Florida State University.

I shoved the throttle forward and felt the aircraft accelerate. It was late on a Friday afternoon in 1986 and I was concluding a production test flight on a navy A-7 attack jet. As a production test pilot at Naval Air Station Jacksonville, Florida (Navy Jax), I was preparing for the overhead break (high-speed pass) used by jets arriving at the field for entry into the landing pattern.

I had flown this mission profile hundreds of times before, but this time, I felt a little different. As I rolled into a turn overhead the airfield, I glanced downward. I saw the familiar crisscrossed runway pattern and adjacent aircraft parking spaces. I marveled at the bright sun glints from the large P-3 patrol aircraft parked on the tarmac. I saw the accustomed H-3 helicopters and the fighter jets all neatly positioned in their respective parking areas. I heard the familiar voices from the control tower issuing me clearance for the overhead break. On this particular day, however, I did not feel as though I was "returning to base," "returning to home plate," or "recovering," as is typically the description for this phase of flight. I felt as though I was arriving *home.*

America is my home. And when I think of home, I think of security, support of family, opportunities for personal growth, and individual achievement. America means freedom, diversity, strength, technology, and the high standard of living that most of us enjoy. What America means most, however, is the manner in which people of all races, cultures, and religions work together for the common good of our country.

A diverse group of individuals routinely put aside inevitable differences and worked together to ensure the success of my navy missions. A larger, more diverse group did likewise to ensure the success of the space missions I later flew as a NASA astronaut. It is this spirit of teamwork, and even family, that I felt that Friday afternoon in 1986. It is this same spirit of family that has become so prevalent throughout America during the aftermath of the terrorist attacks of one year ago.

We Americans can be an individualistic lot. We realize, however, that only through teamwork and brotherhood can we enable America to lead the whole world and, in the words of science fiction writers, "boldly go where no one has gone before." We realize that our true America is not about finances, real estate, race, profession, or position.

America is about togetherness, about family, about *home*.

God bless America.

God bless my home.

WILLIAM SHATNER

William Shatner is an actor who starred as Captain James Kirk on the Star Trek *television show.*

I am Canadian, and as such, standing on my tiptoes, I could dimly make out on the horizon the country that borders mine. We Canadians looked to the States with admiration and goodwill mixed with a dollop of envy.

From the sinecure of Canada we could feel the pulse of America as it alternated between calm and alarm: Pearl Harbor, McCarthy, the Hiss accusations. America twisted between fear, patriotism, and the desire to be fair. As I watched the events unfold on television, I was filled with trepidation about my upcoming trip to New York and whether I would be enveloped in a firestorm of jingoism because I was a resident alien.

But always in the back of my mind was the steadfast core of belief that America would do right and that once again Americans would choose the correct path of fairness, equanimity, and peacefulness.

And so I came to the States. Since that time, I have seen America at its best and at its worst. Constantly, I have understood the truism that is America. Anchored in the precepts of the Constitution, America invariably makes the right choice. It's uncanny that given enough time with the checks and balances that are embedded in that great document, America rights its wrongs. The world has come to see America and Americans for what they really are.

This country is a world leader for many reasons, but mainly because its freedom and its democracy are founded on laws that were set down over two hundred years ago. The Constitution is probably the greatest political document ever written, and those of us who live in this country and enjoy its benefits can only watch with jaw-dropping fascination as we see America twist and turn and switch and move and finally choose its path.

This country needs only time and information to allow its citizens to make the right and decent move. I'm glad to be a part of it.

ARTIE SHAW

Artie Shaw is a former leading jazz clarinetist and big band leader. He led a U.S. Navy big band during World War II.

I've spent close to ninety-two years living in God knows how many different places, including five years in Spain, where I even built a house on a mountainside overlooking the Mediterranean where I expected to live for the rest of my life. . . . However, for reasons too convoluted to go into here, I ultimately ended up in California. After all that, I can only say that this amazing nation of ours, despite all its disparate social problems—and, as we know, there are still far too many of those—is still the best country on the face of this troubled planet where an individual can live a halfway reasonable life.

JACKIE W. SHERRILL
Jackie W. Sherrill is head football coach
at Mississippi State University.

On some level, I've always known that I live in the greatest country on the planet, but I don't remember ever taking the time to talk about it. That perspective in itself demonstrates the privilege I have felt as an American.

We, as American citizens, have always been able to *expect* to be safe, *expect* to pursue our dreams, and *expect* to grow old. We are safely cradled in the arms of democracy.

I was in my office on the morning of September 11, 2001. I began the morning as I had for the past thirty-five Septembers of my life; I was preparing to meet an opponent on the football field, only to get a call from my wife, Peggy. With her voice cracking, she said to turn on the television; someone has just flown a plane into the World Trade Center.

I was in shock, in disbelief, in denial, angry that this event had actually taken place, and was crying at the same time.

In all my years in football, I have often heard people liken football to war. Two generals . . . squaring off behind their respective troops. I'll never again hear this analogy in the same way.

Football is just a game, and I am privileged to live in a country where I have the luxury of making it my career. I can use it to do some good in this world and it's being a citizen of this country that affords me that privilege. I am grateful to be a son of the United States of America.

I love this country and the people who make it what it is. God Bless the U.S.A.

PAUL SIMON

Paul Simon is a former United States senator from Illinois, and director of the Public Policy Institute at Southern Illinois University.

We fly an American flag in the front yard of our rural home. I served overseas in the army under that flag. I am proud of what it stands for, and the events of September 11 have not diminished that pride.

We are not a perfect nation. Human beings don't create such things. But we struggle to preserve our freedoms—and do fairly well at that; we strive to give opportunity to all within our boundaries, and we are getting better at that; we are learning to understand the faiths and cultures of new immigrants to our shores.

Most international visitors return to their home countries favorably impressed by the United States.

But just before receiving the invitation of Hugh Downs to contribute to this book I read an article in the Eugene, Oregon, *Register-Guard* written by Michael Rooke-Ley, who has served as a Fulbright professor in Sri Lanka and Croatia. He writes that our image abroad is that we are "young, cocky, rich and powerful." I have visited in more than one hundred nations, and I regret to say that there is some accuracy to his conclusion. Sometimes we have been insensitive to the other 96 percent of the world, and that insensitivity often comes across as arrogance.

I am proud as an American that this nation created the Marshall Plan, a generous act unprecedented in the history of the community of nations. Under the Marshall Plan we led the world in aiding the poor beyond our borders. But I am also aware that as our interest in people beyond our borders has slipped, so have our actions, and now among the twenty-one wealthy nations, we are dead last in the percentage of our income that goes to help the world's desperate. That does not justify the senseless and tragic acts of September 11, but it added to an atmosphere that was not helpful.

During our presidential elections, foreign policy barely gets mentioned because of a lack of public interest. That does not help us.

I am proud that we freely elect our public officials, but I am not proud of the poor turnout in our elections, nor of our way of financing those elections.

My list of things to which I look with pride is long, but I also have a long list of improvements I would like to see.

There is no such thing as preserving the status quo. We either move ahead or fall back. I want us to move ahead.

NANCY SNYDERMAN

Nancy Snyderman, M.D., is medical correspondent for ABC's Good Morning America *and also reports for 20/20.*

September 11, 2001, I was stuck. Standing in the Denver International Airport at 7 A.M. waiting to board my flight to New York City, I watched the horror of that day unfold on television. My body, my psyche, was swept with confusion, grief, terror, and the primal need to flee.

But where could I go? As a reporter and a doctor I knew I needed to be in New York. But that was now a physical impossibility. I called the rim–the pulse of ABC News–to find out what was going on. The answer was painfully obvious. We were under attack. I pulled a gate agent from United Airlines aside, introduced myself, and told her what I knew. Her face froze. I knew more than those behind the counters.

As an American, uncertain as to whether this was a first wave of attacks, I wanted to get away from large groups of people. With the airport beginning to move people to a "secured concourse," I wanted out. I talked a Denver woman standing near me into getting her car from the parking lot and driving me back to my hotel in downtown Denver. Years before I had hitched a ride on a cargo plane to get out of Somalia, so I figured I could find a way to get out of Denver International Airport.

The weekend before had started as innocently as anyone else's. I attended an annual medical meeting with my father and brother, also surgeons. This was now a rite of passage and a time of the year that we very much enjoyed. A father, second-generation American, and his two children sharing our medical careers together.

I spent the hours after the attack as so many did— glued to the TV watching the scenes over and over again and coming to the realization that we would be forever transformed. For hours I cried, tracked down friends, kept in touch with ABC News (in case there were other attacks across the country), and hugged everyone in sight. My insides had been scooped out. I was numb. How could anyone hate us this much? Why now? Why there?

But while I was stuck and so frustrated for not being in New York where I should have been reporting or helping the injured (which tragically never turned out to be a need), I was also stuck far from home. My three children were back in San Francisco. My daughters, fifteen and thirteen, had been to the World Trade Center. They knew the buildings and the café on the plaza. I knew I had to get home. With no flights, no trains, and not a rental car to be had, I flipped into disaster mode.

I opened the phone book and started looking for car dealerships. I had flirted with the idea of getting a new truck for our ranch when I got back home. Now, I would just buy it sooner and in another state. Only one thing had changed. I could not foresee what would happen to us. Would there be other attacks? Would we have fuel shortages and gas rationing? One thing I knew the government couldn't do was shut down long-haul truck drivers—so a diesel pickup truck would be the choice. There was only one in the entire Denver area. Five Chevy truck lots and only one diesel, and it had my name on it.

At 9 P.M. September 12 my parents and I took a cab to the dealership. There was no bargaining. Ten-twenty P.M. and the three of us were driving out in a Chevy diesel long-bed pickup truck. I had never driven anything so big. But I knew that I could find diesel fuel on Interstate 80, and if push came to shove I could take the four-wheel drive on back roads or through someone's field. Nothing was going to stop me from getting home.

My father thought I had lost my mind. He had been through World War II and knew how fast Americans would scramble. "We'll have air marshals tomorrow," he said, "and beside, I want to get back to Indianapolis, not go west to San Francisco." I was not as optimistic and tried to tell him he wasn't going anywhere. I told my mom and dad that Thursday morning I was driving home to San Francisco and they could join me if they wanted to. This would be a wonderful chance to see the grandchildren. I felt like a caged animal and I was going to move.

At 5:30 the next morning I was standing at the truck and they appeared. My father told me it wasn't safe for me to go by myself, my mother smiled, and we all knew we just wanted to be together.

The next twenty hours were one of the greatest gifts ever given to me. I drove across Colorado, Wyoming, Utah, Nevada, and California. I was transfixed by the purple mountains (yes, they are purple) and stunned by the raw beauty of the plains. Even if someone hated us, the people, how could anyone hate her, this glorious country? The three of us talked and cried and had hours of silence. We spoke of Europe before my father's family settled here, and I heard stories about their lives during World War II that I had never heard before. We listened to the service at the National Cathedral and were somehow glad we shared this through the power of radio. The words and the sounds painted their own pictures.

I was on a road trip with two of the greatest people, two of the finest Americans I have ever known. They taught me that I could be anything I wanted to be when I grew up; I shouldn't feel shackled by other people's expectations nor those of society's. They preached kindness and respect and tolerance and responsibility. And they lived those very ideals.

As the miles clicked by, we spoke of many things, but the common denominator was repeatedly how proud and lucky we were to be Americans and that we would see ourselves through this.

I thought back to my childhood and the day our local newspaper printed the headline in red during the Cuban Missile Crisis. I was terrified and my fear was just reinforced every time we had to hide under a desk during a disaster drill. Would I drive home to the same fears in my children?

I had plenty of time to prepare myself, and hundreds of American flags from overpasses, semitrailers, police cars, and front yards bolstered my love of country. My beliefs were strong and my job would be to make my children understand my convictions and at the same time make them feel secure. Seeing their faces, having their arms around my neck, was the final act of my treasured twenty hours. Through this nation's tragedy I was given a gift: I was given the gift of time to link one generation to another and another, and bridge them with the strength and optimism that it means to be an American.

The wet blanket of sadness hasn't left me yet. I cry at odd times and I have been to ground zero more than once. But this American will raise her children much as I was raised by my World War II parents—with love of country, love of the earth, and sheer optimism for tomorrow. After all, isn't that distinctly American?

MARY SOJOURNER

Mary Sojourner is a writer, NPR commentator, environmental activist, and author of the new essay collection, Bonelight: Ruin and Grace in the New Southwest. *She lives in an old cabin near Flagstaff, Arizona.*

I write from the heart of imperfect sanctuary. It is just past noon on the first day of the year 2002. Sun warms my face. The dark forest floor is patched with snow and shadow. I sit in the center of what, for many decades, was a cluster of seven ponderosa pine. The seventh trunk, the one we called the Gatekeeper, was cut five years ago—who knows why?

I've just scattered crackers for the ravens and Steller's jays who have fed and yakita-yakked here far longer than my species. I am in the country I love; in a high desert pine forest on the edge of a mountain town whose population has doubled in twelve years; in a state whose deserts and rare wetlands have been eaten alive by development; in a nation no longer able to imagine it is invulnerable— or alone.

This is land of inherent meaning. It is not "my" America. Rather, I am a guest here, in huge places of pale sage and dark volcanic ranges; in little pockets of bright air as fragile and vital as the connection between yucca and moth; in places beyond description because they change as the vast western light changes, all places I will not name—for their own protection.

These places teach me. They insist, as I enter them on foot, without four-wheel drive or cell phone, without signal flare or GPS, on my respect. They remind me that I am both tiny and insatiable. Free as breath and responsible as the love I feel for them.

And, in the long run, essential and temporary as a rattler's track across the bare sand of an unnamed desert wash.

BILLY SQUIER

Billy Squier is a musician.

DECEMBER 25, 2001, NEW YORK CITY

On the morning of September 11, workers at the World Trade Center—led by metro firefighters and police—were called upon to demonstrate their courage and commitment to the city they called home. Their unflinching response (and ultimate sacrifice) will resonate forever throughout the annals of history.

America staggered, but did not fall.

In the aftermath of unprecedented tragedy, Americans of *all* ages and means responded in kind—contributing time and money, thoughts and prayers . . . in a relief effort that is unparalleled in modern times.

In October, Yankee Stadium was sold out for the World Series.

Today, American families, in time-honored national tradition, celebrate the joys of Christmas . . . while the decoration of choice for the season remains the American flag—"Old Glory," which appears practically anyplace you can imagine, and now more than ever symbolizes the pride of a nation and the unity of its people.

It's good to be home.

MAUREEN STAPLETON

Maureen Stapleton is a Tony and Academy Award-winning actress.

Of all the *bad* things that happen to us—poverty, sickness, loss of loved ones, old age, pain, failure, mistakes, hurting someone, disasters, killings—one *good* thing stays the same for us: the goodness of our country.

JOHN STOSSEL

John Stossel is an ABC News correspondent for 20/20, *and anchor and correspondent for* The John Stossel Specials.

America is freedom. Openness. Opportunity.

The founders gave us a few simple rules. What a difference it made.

Their vision was *limited* government: a government that keeps the peace, but otherwise leaves us alone to our free choices. This lack of central planning allowed a "spontaneous order" to flourish. That, plus our central openness and tolerance for oddballs, created the freest, richest, most vital society ever.

How sad that despite America's demonstrated success, *most* people on the earth live in *desperate* conditions, eking out a brutal life, and dying young.

Why? It's so unfair. We *know* what works! It's not speculation anymore. The rules that created America work. Limited government, rule of law, and economic freedom.

Limited government is key, but not sufficient. Millions live in misery because nations don't have *enough* government. Entrepreneurship cannot thrive when people cannot keep the fruits of their labor. Why build a factory if you don't know whether your neighbors or your government will simply take it from you? The poorest nations of the world lack the rule of law that protects private property.

Economic freedom is also key. Canada's Frazier Institute ranks countries by economic freedom. At the bottom of the list are Myanmar, Algeria, Congo, Guinea-Bissau, Sierra Leone, and other countries dominated by government planning. Invariably, these are the worst places to live.

At the top of the rankings are Hong Kong, Singapore, New Zealand, the United Kingdom, and the United States. The countries with the economic freedom are the best places to live.

Freedom isn't everything. Climate matters, religion, geography, even luck can make a difference. But nothing matters as much as liberty, and liberty made America great.

MAIRÉID SULLIVAN

Mairéid Sullivan is an Irish-born singer, song-writer, poet, and writer.

AMERICA–A GOLDEN AGE FOR THE HUMAN SPIRIT

The Golden Age of the American spirit began as a unique experiment for humanity: the first truly multicultural country, populated by people of every nation and tribe. America represents the first society in human history founded upon diverse cultures living together as one people–Americans.

Americans share a tremendous pride in their ancestry, celebrating each side of the family tree equally, going back before their ancestors first settled this wide, majestic land.

America's achievement is founded on a cultural rejuvenation unprecedented in human history; a renaissance, facilitated by communication technology, inspired by the idea of unity in diversity–the cross-pollination of diverse cultural heritage.

Thomas Jefferson, who was known as a man of the people, wrote in the Declaration of Independence, "We hold these truths to be self-evident, that all men are created equal." Jefferson also believed in a "wise and frugal Government, which shall restrain men from injuring one another," while encouraging its citizens to freely manage their own affairs.

The Bill of Rights is the legal foundation for our liberties, but the Declaration of Independence is, I think, more reflective of the philosophy of the founders of this country.

American multicultural society has not had an easy transition. Generations of Americans, indigenous and immigrant, continue to overcome profound tragedies while coming to terms with their differences.

The achievement of peaceful cohabitation within American society is based on the awareness that all people are kindred in spirit. For Americans of every faith, their experience of infinite divine life goes hand-in-hand with their sense of duty to nurture the freedom the human spirit requires to experience irrepressible love and joy.

Americans are capable of helping to maintain the greatest Golden Age of peace the world has ever known, for themselves and for the whole world.

Benjamin Franklin said, "Man will ultimately be governed by God or tyrants." It takes great courage to embrace freedom, to make our own choices, to be leaders of our own lives rather than followers.

The time has come for us to renew our commitment to the spirit of freedom and joy, as we celebrate what has already been achieved for the good of all life, on earth, as it is in heaven.

KAREN TATES-DENTON

Karen Tates-Denton is a production manager at Fine Communications.

Before 9/11 if someone had asked me what nationality I was, I would say, "I am an African American!" If someone asked me on 9/12, I would say, "Because my spirit has been lifted, my eyes have been opened, and my heart has been touched, I am an American!"

Today I feel a sense of what it truly feels like to be an American—to be inclusive on the landscape of America. It is indeed awe-inspiring. I finally feel the emotion behind what it means to stand up and proclaim my Americanism—if there is such a word for it. I often ask myself, "Can feelings translate into being?"

I hope the sentiments of 9/11 give value and credence to a whole segment of people across the country who have never felt "American." People like myself who now feel that they can never go back to just feeling/being other than American. I now feel that I am American not only because of birth and right but because it is a pure, gut emotion that I can no longer deny. I want to value this feeling—this being—not because there is suddenly another shade of brown skin to hate, but because this identity is now an honor. My values, my morals, my choices, my rights, my ancestral contributions are what are American and what typifies America.

How long will I feel a part of it? How long will I feel so intensely about this land? I don't know, but right now, today, no one can take that away from me.

Before 9/11 for all of my years I considered myself an African American. But today, because my spirit has been lifted, my eyes have been opened, and my heart has been forever touched, I am an American.

EDWARD TELLER

Dr. Edward Teller is a noted physicist, director emeritus of Lawrence Livermore National Laboratory, and senior research fellow at the Hoover Institution. He served as assistant director of Los Alamos Scientific Laboratory during World War II.

I was born in Budapest, Hungary, ninety-four years ago and have been a citizen of the United States for more than half a century. I have lived through the First World War as a child, the Second World War, the Cold War, and a decade of hot peace as a participant.

The killing of three thousand people could have received one of the obvious answers: Play down the events or use maximum retaliation. The first would have been absurd; the second would cause a billion Muslims to fight us. Instead we chose a remarkable compromise: Save no effort in responding; at the same time, be careful to avoid excesses.

Indeed, the role the United States has played in the last century has defeated militarism and emptied the concentration camps.

The world has become smaller, and, as a consequence, it is both full of danger and of positive developments.

Our response has been welcomed by the great majority of American people. Even the weakest link in our public affairs, the sensation-hungry press, behaved in an admirable manner.

The administration's decisions and the people's response are the two reasons why I am proud to be a Hungarian-born, 100 percent American.

HELEN THOMAS

*Helen Thomas is a columnist for Hearst News-
papers and a White House correspondent. She
is the author of* Dateline: White House *and*
Thanks for the Memories, Mr. President.

I was very lucky to be born in America, and in my
big family we always thanked the good Lord that
our father, George Thomas, did not miss the boat.
He left his home in Tripoli, Syria, now Tripoli,
Lebanon, in the 1890s as a teenager. He had only a
few cents in his pocket and a talisman containing
the traveler's prayer in Arabic around his neck. He
settled in Winchester, Kentucky, and later returned
to Tripoli, married my mother, and returned to the
U.S.A. in 1903. They had nine children who lived.
In 1924, my family moved to Detroit, where I grew
up, went to public schools, Wayne State University,
and then on to Washington to seek a career in journalism.

In all my years I will marvel at the courage of my
parents. They could not speak the language in their
newly adopted country when they arrived, nor
could they read. But they brought with them great
values of the Arabic culture and they learned to
treasure the unique advantage of living in a democracy and in freedom where their children could be
what they wanted to be. We were never hyphenated
as Arab-Americans. We were American, and I have
always rejected the hyphen and believe all assimi-

lated immigrants should not be designated ethnically. Or separated, of course, by race, or creed either.

These are the trends that ever try to divide us as a people. I love the fact that we are a melting pot. President Franklin D. Roosevelt brought down the house when he addressed the DAR with the salutation: "Fellow Immigrants."

America is great because it cherishes freedom above all for all its people. We are not in castes or classes. We have the Bill of Rights, and especially the First Amendment, which guarantees freedom of religion, speech, the press, assembly, and petition.

This country is also great because it is a nation of laws not men. And no man is above the law. Presidents have found that out when they breached the line. We are not perfect. We have a way to go before we have true equality at the workplace. I personally am still outraged that women did not get the vote in this country until 1920, and then only after the suffragists marched for thirty years. But blacks had it much worse, not getting their full voting rights until 1965.

The country is also great because we have a basically caring society, wanting every child to be educated and no one to starve or lack for medicine, I hope.

All that said, it is my good fortune to have been born here, and it makes me even more determined to help others along the way. True American patriots are tolerant and reject the hubris of fleeting military might.

We should not submit to an atmosphere of fear or give away any of the profound rights that the Founding Fathers bestowed on us in a magnificent legacy. Freedom is not negotiable.

DICK THORNBURGH

Dick Thornburgh has served as governor of the state of Pennsylvania, attorney general of the United States, and under-secretary-general of the United Nations.

Times of crisis provide an opportunity to focus on essentials. Surely, this is true of America in the wake of the dreadful events of September 11, 2001. We have been reminded anew of the differences between the rule of law and the rule of force. We have taken renewed strength from the principled responses of our leaders. We have come to appreciate even more the blessings of freedom, liberty, and democracy that we too often take for granted.

Our history is replete with victories over adversaries of seeming superior strength—in our War for Independence, our Civil War, and two world wars. Today we face enemies of a different character— enemies who parade under a false banner of religious principle, who target innocent civilians and seek to spread death and destruction indiscriminately throughout the civilized world. Although the challenge differs, our response must be the same. We must be resolute in our determination to prevail, sustained by the rightness of our cause, and persistent in the assertion of those principles of human dignity, justice, and individual worth that have served us so well in centuries past.

Tragedy can beget determined response and a commitment to better ourselves, our communities, and our nation in countless ways. Every American now has a role in that response and must share a portion of that commitment. Each of us, in the exercise of the precious rights that we have accumulated over more than two centuries of our history, must resolve to emulate those patriots who have gone before us by remaining steadfast in the defense and propagation of all that is good about our nation and our way of life.

Let our legacy to future generations be that we stood ready at the ramparts during a time of trial and testing, and furthered the greatness that is the U.S.A.

DONALD TRUMP

Donald Trump is president, chairman, and CEO of Trump Hotels and Casino Resorts.

I view this country as being intelligent and brave. To my mind, this is a fortuitous and unbeatable combination. To be brave without intelligence can result in fanaticism. To be intelligent without bravery can render a country powerless. Our country is successful because we have a balance of both of these attributes. We are able to be civilized and successful at once. And that is why we are number one. Few other countries, or empires, in world history can boast of this combination.

I am not only proud to be an American, but extremely grateful to have had the good fortune of being born in this country. That alone is an enviable position to many peoples of the world, and I never lose sight of that fact. No matter how bad things might be, I will always feel lucky. This country is a no-lose situation. Being here is equal to being a winner. Americans who don't feel this way obviously haven't given their situation enough thought.

It took an act of depravity and spiritual destitution to awaken us to our great good fortune as Americans. It also reminded us of how brave we can be, and how adaptable we must be in the face of changing circumstances. As most people know, I have always loved building tall buildings. Sadly, that will have to change. But I will continue building beautiful and strong buildings because they are a reflection of what this country is, and what it represents to me.

There are times when talk is cheap. Actions bring motivation to the surface. This country will not be stopped. I will not be stopped. And I think our strength and pride have been made evident to the world without having to say one single word. And that is saying something.

STANSFIELD TURNER

Admiral Stansfield Turner (USN-Ret.) is a senior research scholar at the Center for International and Security Studies at the University of Maryland. He served as commander of the U.S. Second Fleet and NATO Striking Fleet Atlantic, and as the commander in chief of NATO's Southern Flank. He was director of the CIA from 1977 to 1981.

For me, the United States of America stands first and foremost for freedom and opportunity for the individual. The most important development in the world over the past century has been the vast improvement in respect for the rights of human beings. The United States is the most important factor in this seminal trend. Our leadership in that direction is more important to the long-term well-being of humankind than any of our other numerous accomplishments as a nation.

GRETA VAN SUSTEREN

Greta Van Susteren is host of Fox News Channel's
On the Record with Greta Van Susteren.

In short, but ever so apparent, September 11 changed everything. In the matter of minutes, the terrorists caused unimaginable heartbreak for thousands. Words are inadequate to describe the evil imposed upon innocent people, so I won't begin to try. At the same time the terrorists inflicted their evil upon us, they also instantly exposed what a strong nation the U.S.A. is. Their attack was sudden—but so was our resolve to be united, and united we are. The terrorists have made a huge mistake—they have unleashed the powerful and unlimited will of the American people. We are a determined people, and they will feel it.

JESSE VENTURA

Jesse Ventura is governor of the state of Minnesota and a former professional wrestler.

I view my country in pretty simple terms: It's the greatest on earth and I would do anything asked to defend it.

Why is America the greatest? The obvious answer is our freedom, but I think it goes deeper than that. I think it has to do with the freedom to have our own opinions and the freedom to express them.

You don't like our country? You're free to say that.

You want to burn the flag? You bought it; it's your right to do whatever you want with it.

You don't want to say the Pledge of Allegiance? No one can force you to. You can show your allegiance any way you'd like, or you can choose not to.

Fortunately, you're also free to wave the flag, object to flag burning, and say the pledge if that's how you want to express your patriotism.

I've been all over the world, and I can tell you firsthand that when it comes to freedom, there is just no another place in the world like our country.

THOMAS J. VILSACK

Thomas J. Vilsack is governor of the state of Iowa.

"Our liberties we prize," says the motto of my state of Iowa, "and our rights we will maintain."

It is those liberties and those rights—long taken for granted by most of us—that the September 11 terrorists tried to blow up. And it is those liberties and those rights that survived that frightful day.

That is the strength of America, and that is what America means to me. On September 10, the people of America could say what they wanted to say, print what they wanted to print, worship where they wanted to worship, assemble where they wanted to assemble. On September 12, they still could. Buildings were smashed, and people were killed—an awfulness that no person will ever forget—but our liberties and our rights proved indestructible.

Democracy is always being tested. Warriors and terrorists try to smash it; hate mongers and tyrants try to subvert it. Yet time and again the people of America have shown that the Constitution they cherish cannot be smashed, the government they believe in cannot be subverted. The tests are horrible—sometimes, unspeakably so—yet democracy survives.

Once more, it has been tested. Once more, it has survived.

We have maintained our rights. So, still, we can prize our liberties.

MORT WALKER

Mort Walker is creator of the "Beetle Bailey" comic strip, and, with Dik Browne, "Hi and Lois."

MIKE WALLACE

Mike Wallace is senior correspondent on CBS's 60 Minutes. *He has served as coeditor of* 60 Minutes *since its premiere in 1968 and worked in radio with Hugh Downs.*

I guess it was out in the Western Pacific in World War II that I first began to feel myself emotionally an American. I'd come up from Fremantle, West Australia, to Subic Bay in the Philippines serving as a communications officer aboard the submarine tender USS *Anthedon,* and I began to hear at first-hand and from the submariners coming back off their war patrols tales of what they'd been through as the U.S. finally began to take the Japanese war machine apart. I felt a vicarious pride in their American courage—and success. I was twenty-six.

Up to that time I'd always taken my country for granted. I was American and happy about it, that was a given. Satisfied that it was the best of all countries, and that I was especially fortunate because my parents had come here as Russian immigrants at the turn of the century and were given the opportunity, the freedom to work and earn a proper living, to send their kids to good public schools and to be free from the prejudice that had marked their Russian lives.

We lived in Brookline, Massachusetts, not far from where the Kennedys lived in a similarly modest house. Young Jack and I went to the same public school, Edward Devotion, along with our friend Masao Yatsuhashi, whose family had immigrated from Japan, and young Andrew Plakias from Greece. In my teens our president was Franklin Roosevelt, a hero to my parents, therefore to me and to most of the families we knew. He was ours, we felt; on our side. And America was the land of opportunity, where anything or just about anything was possible.

It's almost seventy years later now and as I contemplate America today—as my old friend Hugh Downs has asked me to—and ask myself what my country means to me, I find myself astonished, really, at how little my perceptions have changed.

This country has had its tail twisted over and over again during these seventy years: wars, depression, scandals, racial hurt, terrorism, corruption, bigotry, all of it. And I've been lucky enough to have had the chance to see a lot of it close up, and to have covered it first for radio and then for television, to have suffered personally from some of it and come out the other side mainly unscarred.

What I've come away with, especially having traveled much of the world during the past half century and having seen other countries, other peoples close-up, is that America remains, despite its various well-catalogued shortcomings, an inspiration to those who are born here or who have come here to share in its opportunities, or who yearn from overseas to have the same chances we've been granted.

Somehow, despite all, we survive and flourish. Faced with disasters, body blows like those we suffered on 9/11, we find the leaders, the laborers, the guts, the Americans to honor who we are and where we've come from.

America to me is still what it used to be when I was a youngster. It is courage, energy, resourcefulness, determination. Too much materialism sometimes, insufficient kindness, the callousness of a people in a hurry, and too often a smug sense of superiority.

But at rock bottom, it's a helluva country, and I'm proud I'm one of us.

Barbara Walters

Barbara Walters, host of the Barbara Walters specials, is cohost and coanchor of ABC's The View, *as well as ABC News correspondent and coanchor of* 20/20. *Barbara Walters and Hugh Downs worked as colleagues in broadcasting for thirty-eight years.*

On September 5, 2001, six days before September 11, the new season of *20/20* began. On that date, I aired a startling interview with the actress Anne Heche, who, up until then, was best known for her lesbian relationship with Ellen DeGeneres. In my interview, Anne Heche revealed to the world that she'd thought she was from another planet and had considered herself insane. *20/20* is a newsmagazine and, boy, was this considered news! Sensational and a ratings grabber. What a great fall debut for the program!

I was next about to interview the singer Mariah Carey, who was herself making headlines because she, too, was having emotional problems. This was what most Americans wanted to see, to hear, and to read about—celebrities—actors, singers, models. Almost no one cared about foreign news. Terrorists lived in other countries. Afghanistan was so remote as to be all but off the map.

One week later, September 11!

Amid the tragedy, the devastation, the fear, the

loss of lives, the hideous reality of terrorism in our own country, those of us in the news business were once again in the *real* news business. And we desperately wanted to do our business. We worked day and night, and the stories of victims and their families engulfed us. At one point that week, I talked to the chef and owner of Windows on the World, the famous restaurant on top of the World Trade Center. He sobbed as he tried to count up the many dead and missing of his employees. And we talked on camera with family members of the kitchen staff who had worked the early hours. Some were immigrants, relatively new to this country they had so desired to live in. Virtually all clutched pictures of their loved ones. "Have you seen my sister . . . my husband . . . my son?" We showed their photographs with aching hearts. Stories like these dominated the airwaves, along with investigations and the growing awareness of a man named Osama bin Laden.

That week and the months that followed affected me professionally and personally in the deepest possible way. As it has with so many others, it made me think.

Why did it take a tragedy to make us realize how much we need the security of our home—its comfort, its protection?

Why did the realization that all we thought secure is not make us cherish what we had before so taken for granted?

Why did it take the knowledge of the spiritual treasure we could lose to make us aware of how unimportant material treasures are?

But it did. Now everything has changed. Nothing will ever be the same. And that Anne Heche interview seems a million years ago.

TINA WESSON

Tina Wesson is a nurse and the winner of the CBS adventure series, Survivor 2: The Australian Outback.

I enjoy writing, but when I try to describe what America means to me, the words are hard to come by and they seem inadequate. This is a bit like describing how I feel about my children, whom I love fiercely (with the full intensity of my heart) and unconditionally (even when they do something that upsets me). Although I can try to explain my love, the words only scratch the surface of my profound emotions. So it is with America.

Our country has been wounded. It seems smaller and suddenly vulnerable. Our child is not invincible, and though that causes us pain and fear, we must rally our protective instincts and take care of America. And I believe America will only grow stronger from this adversity. I've always loved patriotic tunes, and now when I sing, with hand over my heart, "for the land of the free and the home of the brave," I often find tears on my cheeks. When I sing, "God shed his grace on thee," I feel His abundant grace all around. "Oh beautiful, for spacious skies" brings to mind the wonderful images from across this scenic nation, images I have gathered in a land where I can be free.

Lacking the language to fully define my passion for America, let me just say my country lives in me.

I hope it lives in you, too.

CURTIS WILKIE

Curtis Wilkie is a journalist and the author of Dixie: A Personal Odyssey Through Events That Shaped the Modern South.

For me, love of country has been a long, turbulent romance filled with upset and passion, anger, and, finally, grateful appreciation.

At first, patriotism seemed as wholesome as a diet of dairy products. My childhood took place in the 1940s, a time of rich promise. Our nation had conquered the Great Depression and emerged as a global power after World War II. I have a distant memory of waving a tiny American flag as the returning heroes marched in parade, and being taught to be thankful for our abundance.

Then, with my adolescence came disruption. In my native territory, the Deep South, a chorus of rebellion rose up against our national government. We were asked to hold allegiance to a confederacy dead for nearly a century rather than recognize the federal courts and Congress; to fly a beaten battle flag instead of the star-spangled banner. In their effort to prolong the life of Jim Crow, our regional leaders—crying "states rights"—depicted the United States as the enemy, and for years our relationship with our country was strained.

Because America is good, America eventually broke the back of official segregation and brought us back into the fold.

But for many Americans—in all sections of the country—another rupture occurred when the faraway war in Vietnam came home. Those who raised questions about U.S. military policies were accused of being "un-American"; we were made to feel estranged. While pursuing the war overseas, the administration captured the American flag as its political poster at home. As a result, I felt uncomfortable with the flag for years. And to me, that particular president of the United States personified Samuel Johnson's words, "Patriotism is the last refuge of a scoundrel."

Though troubled, I was never prepared to break with my country. We had our own popular antiwar poster in those days that conveyed the thoughts of my conflicted state of mind. I hung it on my wall. "I should like," the poster's wistful message said, "to love my country and still love justice."

Then the war ended, hostilities at home ebbed, and I eventually resumed my love affair with my country. I traveled the world, lived overseas for years in my job as a journalist, and discovered—just as did Dorothy after visiting Oz—that there's no place like home.

Despite my ups and downs and lingering doubts about patriotism, I never ceased being an American.

But how terrible it is, I think now, that it took the tragedy of September to make me consider, at last, how valuable my country is to me.

ROGER WILLIAMS

Roger Williams is a celebrated pianist who has recorded more than 115 albums.

I can sum up my feelings about this great country of ours in three words—*compared to what?*

I joined the navy in World War II. Boot camp and officers' training toughened me up in a way I wish all young Americans could experience today. And, we didn't mind. After Pearl Harbor, most of us couldn't wait to enlist. It took nearly sixty years until I saw that same kind of spirit in America again. Hallelujah! Now when I travel the world—*compared to what*—I come home and kiss the ground!

DAN WOODING

Dan Wooding is an award-winning journalist and author. He and his wife, Norma, founded ASSIST (Aid to Special Saints in Strategic Times), a missionary organization.

A TRIP INTO TERROR AND LOVE

It was on Tuesday, September 11, while we were in Gerasa (Jerash), the most complete and best-preserved Greco-Roman city in the Middle East, when we first heard the news that all hell had broken loose in New York City.

I was with a team of twenty-eight American Christian leaders and journalists when one of our team, Giles Hudson, received a mobile phone call from an American Christian news network in Dallas, Texas, telling him that a plane had slammed into one of the twin towers of the World Trade Center.

In a state of shock, we walked to the nearby city of Gadara (modern Um Qais), with its spectacular panoramic views overlooking the Sea of Galilee, the site of Jesus' miracle of the Gadarene swine, where He sent demented spirits out of two men into a herd of swine who ran down the hill and drowned in the Sea of Galilee (Matthew 8:28–34), and there we received more information about the second plane crashing into another of the towers. It was as if the demons of hate had been unleashed on America and all we could do was to pray for the victims and their relatives.

It was surreal to be in Jordan at the time of the worst terrorist attack in world history. Very soon, we were overwhelmed with Jordanian people who stopped us at every place we went to offer their condolences.

Before we left for a candlelight service with nearly five hundred Jordanian Christians and Muslims, a bellboy at our hotel in Amman asked if he could address us on the bus's PA system. He told us that he had lost some of his family in the fighting in the West Bank and said that he knew what it was to lose members of his family that he loved. "I would like to tell you that I am very sorry for what has happened in America, and I want you to know that all of the Jordanian people share in your sorrow."

We then joined with others in lighting candles for peace at a special candlelight remembrance service at the Citadel in Amman on Sunday, September 16, to show solidarity with the victims and their families of the New York and Washington terrorist attacks on the World Trade Center and the Pentagon.

Muslim clerics united with Christian priests and ministers from the various Christian communities in Jordan, as well as the lord mayor of Amman, in condemning the violence in the United States and praying for the families of the victims. It was hard for us to hold back the tears at this momentous time in world history.

After the service, our team headed for Amman Airport, to fly back to New York on Royal Jordanian Airlines on what turned out to be the first flight from an Arab country. Security was tight and we understood that several armed marshals were on the flight. We were told later that when we arrived in American airspace, we were escorted to JFK Airport by three fighter jets.

When we arrived at the airport, a bevy of armed FBI agents and other security met us. Like many, I couldn't catch the flight I was booked on and so had to find another airline to get back to southern California. As we took off, I could see the pall of smoke rising from what had been the twin towers of the World Trade Center.

Like all of us who are proud to be Americans, I will never forget what has happened to our world over those few days. It was heartening to know that so many from around the world are standing with the American people in love and solidarity and, like our friends in Jordan, are lighting symbolic candles for peace.

DAVID WRIGHT

David Wright is an ABC News correspondent. He files reports for World News Tonight with Peter Jennings, Good Morning America, *and* World News Saturday/Sunday.

On my last day in Afghanistan, the marines raised a flag at Kandahar Airport, sent there by the New York Police Department. Each star was inscribed with a name—police officers killed September 11, sailors killed aboard the USS *Cole.* New Yorkers had signed the stripes of the flag, which had flown at ground zero in the days immediately after the attacks.

For the marines, the Stars and Stripes are a totem of purpose, a reminder of their mission, and in Kandahar this flag had special significance. But I was surprised at how much it meant to me. I had spent the better part of three months in Afghanistan covering the war. This was no ordinary assignment. It was impossible not to take it personally.

I knew little about Afghanistan before September 11, but I immersed myself in the place. We all griped about missing the comforts of home—flush toilets, a bed to sleep on, a hot bath, paved roads—but the truth is none of that mattered. Covering this story forced us to experience firsthand the struggle of daily life in that part of the world, and we felt privileged to be there.

Among our translators, there was a soft-spoken young man from Kabul named Arian Mouj. When we met him, he was saving up his money to emigrate—illegally, if necessary—anywhere he could go. Later, after witnessing the war with us, he decided he wanted to be a journalist. Every night, he would listen to the broadcast, writing down the words that he didn't understand so he could ask us about them the following morning.

Arian is educated and intelligent. He is resourceful too, having survived months behind bars in a Taliban jail. (He was imprisoned because he had trimmed his beard.) He is one of the most honest people I have ever met. And he's only twenty-two, about the same age as many of those marines at Kandahar Airport.

Unlike them, Arian's opportunities are limited by an accident of birth. Despite his many gifts, he faces the daunting obstacle of having lived his entire life in a state of war and, for the last few years, under a regime that practically outlawed dreams. Because the Stars and Stripes now fly over Kandahar, his chances are a bit better.

If only, I keep wishing, he could see New York.

LUCY YANG

Lucy Yang is a general assignment reporter with WABC-TV New York Eyewitness News.

AMERICA ... SO BEAUTIFUL

One's first love is never forgotten. As an immigrant, I knew at an early age that my heart belonged to America. Even before boys, clothes, and shopping, I began my love affair with this great nation.

I was two when we touched down on U.S. soil. I had a seat on my mother's lap as we flew over the Pacific Ocean, then journeyed cross-country aboard a Greyhound bus. We joined my father in Chicago, where he had already started his medical training and where we were to begin our story.

I spoke to all in Taiwanese; they returned the conversation with smiles and nods. I knew I would love this country.

Today, I speak English for a living. As a television journalist in New York City, I have interviewed heroes and villains, victims and victors.

In 1993 a ship called the *Golden Venture* came too close to shore and ran aground in the Far Rockaways. She was filled with the desperate from the Fukian Province of China, who willingly sold their souls for a chance in America. Agreeing to the smuggler's ransom, they knew the sun would set on their working days before their debt was extinguished, but they believed the sun would rise anew for their children. The captain, fearful of getting caught, pushed his passengers into the ocean. Within sight of their promised land, their dreams vanished in the waves. I remember those souls every November, when I cast my vote.

Legions continue to flock to the promise within our borders. Some flee poverty, others persecution. The attraction of America was so compelling that my family abandoned wealth and political power to start anew. It matters not from whence we came; we all seek the same gift . . . freedom.

Once upon a time, not long ago but a world away, I could gaze at the twin towers through my windows. I would glance at them nightly before turning the page on another day, and the blinking lights would return my good-night wish. Some need to see their mountain, others their ocean. I embrace the city skyline, though the constellation of lights has dimmed.

As we reflect upon September 11, 2001, some will highlight the horror, the evil, the madness, the anger, and certainly the loss on that tragic day. I will remember the beauty of each victim, fearfully and wonderfully made by God in His image. Whether they toiled downtown to support their families or rushed past fear and flames to define heroism, I pause and thank them posthumously.

On this solemn anniversary, I concentrate not on the valley of the shadow of death, but look beyond to God's grace. Our nation's testimony is that in our greatest hour of need, hearts turned to the Lord, prayers flooded the heavens, and neighbors extended the right hand of compassion. If His blessings are upon us, I fear not for this country, for His angels are posted on our four corners. May there never be an "Amen" to our prayers for one another and for our great nation.

I have other loves now: God, family, and friends. But I will always treasure my first love, America . . . so beautiful.

I suppose it is expected that my closing remarks will summarize (or attempt to top) everything that has come before.

Don't look for it. Not only because I wouldn't try it, but because all these statements about our America have spoken for themselves: eloquently, emotionally, rationally, chastisingly, or with deep personal feeling.

I can only add a postscript of narrative and opinion—which of course is personal.

My wife's parents were both born in Lebanon, but they didn't meet until they were in the United States. My father-in-law arrived here via Mexico with fifty cents in his pocket. He was bright, enterprising, and energetic, and his dream of a better life unfolded as it can only in this country. He finally owned a grocery company. He raised children who knew how to value what the nation stands for. Once, shortly after Ruth and I were married, I mentioned to him that we wanted to go to Lebanon. I meant we wanted to visit Lebanon. He misunderstood and thought I wanted to take his daughter to live there. I remember him exploding, and saying, "One hour in this country is worth ten years over there!" He had the background and experience to realize how lucky we were to be in the United States.

The New World, before a large hunk of it became

the United States of America, presented earlier settlers with challenges and opportunities bigger than had ever been offered humans before: The success of the American experiment is the fulfillment of the European dream. Religious freedom, participation in the government, the rule of law rather than a rule of men, the hope for a good life, and the reasonable chance of handing a better world to progeny—all these things were sought by generations of Europeans, who had enjoyed little success in moving toward them. The English colonies reached that threshold in 1776, and after fighting to hold on to it, formed the most enlightened government the world had seen.

What was the concept that drove the framers of the Constitution to include in that marvelous document all the instruments it would need to safeguard the freedoms, protect progress, provide for course-correction, and promote the idea that the life and liberty of each individual are sacred? (Not just each citizen, but each human on the planet.) It was not, as some think, a religious idea, in spite of the number of times the deity was invoked to bless or approve details. It was derived from no dogma. It was not from the benign impulses of those who were doing the shaping at the moment.

I believe it was from a deep understanding of human nature, and the optimistic view that our human sense of cooperation, empathy, and charity outweigh our greed, ruthlessness, and capacity to hate. (In the news business, because "good news is no news," as the maxim goes, we tend to spotlight the unusual, the sad, the negative—and this breeds a suspicion that human nature is a rather sorry set of characteristics.) The Founding Fathers had a less provincial outlook on human destiny, and carved into law their belief that human nature was basically *good,* and that a good life could be made available to everyone.

The occasional nasty setback can dent our faith in that outlook. The Holocaust, the chronic violence in the Middle East and Northern Ireland, the September 11 terrorist attack and the awareness that followed of the magnitude of the hate that could cause such an outburst, can bring on a panicky reaction that threatens the very values we wish to preserve.

In countering threats of this kind, we risk overreaction, and we occasionally slip over the edge. Roosevelt's herding of innocent Japanese Americans into detention camps after the December 7, 1941, attack on the Hawaiian Naval Base; sedition charges in World War I that imprisoned men and women for mild criticism of the war's conduct; England's Alien and Sedition Act; France's official violence against suspected royalists in 1798; our national paranoia over an imagined monolithic communism that led to ruined careers during the McCarthy era are examples. After the attacks of September 11, 2001, on the World Trade Center and the Pentagon, we moved to detain people without charging them and to try them in military tribunals with secret evidence and without making the proceedings public. The detention of the Taliban and al-Qaeda fighters raised concern among our allies that we might not be humane in our treatment of these prisoners, not declared prisoners of war—particularly since, unlike our European neighbors, we still have a death penalty. Nations now collaring terrorists are reluctant to turn them over to us for this reason.

How can we be optimistic about the future of our country when the news is filled with racial strife, serial murder, political obstructionism, tragedy on the highways, railways, and airways, the apparent disarray of all our institutions, greed and mean-spiritedness—all the things that make headlines? There's hardly a whole day that is free of reports on such things.

But this is the nature of news. A free press automatically gives weight and emphasis to the tragic, the unusual, the sad, the violent, producing a skewed picture of human nature. Human empathy, cooperation, and civilized impulses do not add up to news as a rule. We need to sort some things out for a better understanding. And it would help if news agencies could be more sensitive to the value of perspective in reporting.

What's so great about America? Is it the vastness of our resources? The grandeur of our geography?

The might of our military? The technological leadership and the products we turn out? The power of our academic research and teaching? The democratic traditions that ward off tyranny? The checks and balances that keep our complicated government from unraveling? All of these should be factored into any assessment of the country's greatness.

But the real glory of the nation is the principles that we officially espouse: human rights, the sovereignty of the individual, the freedom to think and speak as we like, the belief that we can continue to move toward and achieve some universal realization of these ideals.

Without these, we would still be mighty . . . but we would not be great.

—Hugh Downs